PENGUIN PLAYS
PL 35
THREE IRISH PLAYS

THREE IRISH PLAYS

Introduced and Edited by

E. MARTIN BROWNE

THE MOON IN THE YELLOW RIVER
Denis Johnston

THE IRON HARP
Joseph O'Conor

STEP-IN-THE-HOLLOW
Donagh MacDonagh

PENGUIN BOOKS

Penguin Books Ltd, Harmondsworth, Middlesex
U.S.A.: Penguin Books Inc., 3300 Clipper Mill Road, Baltimore 11, M l
AUSTRALIA: Penguin Books Pty Ltd, 762 Whitehorse Road,
Mitcham, Victoria

—

Printed in Great Britain by
Western Printing Services Ltd

CONTENTS

INTRODUCTION

In the earlier part of this century, Ireland supplied a quite dispropor-
tionate amount of the best plays written in our language. The Irish
theatre was infused with a power and a poetry sadly lacking in the
English, except when the Irishman G.B.S. invaded it. Three great
masters worked in Dublin: W. B. Yeats as poet and creator of new
theatrical forms, J. M. Synge as the distiller of the essence of Irish
rustic speech and character, and Sean O'Casey doing the same office
for the people of his native Dublin.

Since then – since Ireland has lived an independent life – the cry has
often gone up that the glory has departed from her theatre. The
present volume gives some proof that this is happily not altogether
true. It contains the best-known play of the most gifted writer of the
generation following those referred to above, and two new plays
published here for the first time. All of them belong unmistakably
to the tradition of Irish drama which the great masters initiated;
the richness of their language alone convinces one of this. But they are
rich not only in the use of words but in the life from which the words
spring.

Denis Johnston's *The Moon in the Yellow River* was first produced
at the Abbey Theatre, Dublin, in 1931. The Abbey, supported by the
Irish government as a National Theatre, has not maintained that
imaginative understanding of the Irish genius which characterized
its early years: much of its production has been of a parochially
realistic kind. But in Johnston it found for a time an author who was
able to do for the modern Ireland, faced with the impact of science
and invention upon its ancient way of life, what Yeats and Synge
had done for the older Ireland. He wrote about Dublin herself in *The
Old Lady Says No*, and about the coming of technology to the countryside in this play. Each is the product of a brilliant, subtle and essentially
Irish mind; each of his characters has its own rich eccentricity, and no
facile conclusion is sought for the complex conflicts both of personality
and of ideas.

Joseph O'Conor's *The Iron Harp* is a straightforward tragedy, set in
the time of the Troubles which brought the Irish Republic to birth.

He was born in Dublin in 1916, and came to London to establish him-self as an actor just before the Second World War. After serving in the British forces he returned to London to make a distinguished career, notable events in which have been his playing of Christ in the York Mystery Plays (1951 and 1954) and his leadership of the Bristol Old Vic Company (1956–7). *The Iron Harp* is his first play. It won the Foyle Award for the best new play produced by a 'Rep' in 1955, and was shortly afterwards given at Bristol Old Vic.

Donagh MacDonagh, the author of *Step-in-the-Hollow*, has already been represented once in this series, by *Happy as Larry* in *Four Modern Verse Plays*. He is the son of one of the martyrs in the Easter Rising of 1916, and is a District Judge in the Irish courts. This proves useful as a background of knowledge to the racy tale of a judge who is a good deal more of a rogue than most of those he tries. *Step-in-the-Hollow* is an outrageous farce in the Falstaffian vein, with a hero as amoral, and as funny, though never as touching, as the Fat Knight. It was first staged by Hilton Edwards, who with Michael Mac-Liammoir has for many years provided in his Gate Theatre manage-ment the breath of civilization which the Abbey failed to give, without the loss of any of that exuberant vitality which Irish actors can provide. The play was a great success with Edwards as the judge. It is here printed for the first time. Laughter of the scale evoked by *Step-in-the-Hollow* is rare, and will be enjoyed with gratitude.

E. MARTIN BROWNE

DENIS JOHNSTON

The Moon in the Yellow River

THE MOON IN THE YELLOW RIVER

This play was first presented at the Abbey Theatre, Dublin, on 27 April 1931, with the following cast:

AGNES	Maureen Delany
BLANAID	Shelah Richards
TAUSCH	Fred Johnson
AUNT COLUMBA	Eileen Crowe
GEORGE	Arthur Shields
CAPTAIN POTTS	Michael J. Dolan
DOBELLE	F. J. McCormick
WILLIE	U. Wright
DARRELL BLAKE	Denis O'Dea
COMMANDANT LANIGAN	P. J. Carolan

Produced by Lennox Robinson

The action of the play takes place in an old fort, now used as a dwelling-house, near the mouth of a river in Ireland.

ACT ONE	*The Living Room*
ACT TWO	*The Armoury*
ACT THREE	*The Living Room*

TIME:

The play opens on an evening in late September.
Act Two overlaps Act One by about five minutes.
Several hours elapse between Acts Two and Three.

ACT ONE

The house was once the officers' quarters of the fort covering the river mouth. But it is now a long time since racks of small arms decorated the stone walls, and for a number of years it has done duty as a fairly comfortable, if out-of-the-way, modern residence. The room is furnished sparsely with good heavy furniture upon which the sea air has left its mark, and it is shockingly untidy. A large book-case is filled with books on technical engineering mixed with a hotchpotch of modern and classical literature. A cupboard filled with old blue-prints hangs open, and a small heap of fishing-tackle lies in the corner. To one side of the rear wall the massive door opens on to the court. It still carries some of the relics of its warlike past in the shape of rusty chains and bolts. To the centre the original aperture has been enlarged into a big window with iron shutters, opening outwards and hung with heavy curtains. These now stand open and we can see out and across the court to a whitewashed wall in which is a cannon port. Shortly after the scene opens it grows dark outside. Whenever the hall door is open, the distant hum of turbines can be heard. To one side of the room a short flight of stairs runs up to a gallery, off which the bedrooms open, of which the door of the first is visible. And down towards us, on one side, is an unpainted wooden table, running off stage out of sight, upon which is a toy railway station, signal box, signals and siding and a set of tracks which emerge from an aperture and disappear again.

[As the Curtain rises a ship's siren can be heard from the river. It is an evening in late September, and an enormous red-faced woman wearing an apron is laying a few plates on the centre table. Although she has strong, domineering eyes and a commanding voice, there is nothing masculine about her. Quite the reverse, for her ample breasts and figure bear witness to a triumphant, all-enveloping matriarchy. Through the open door

[*of the first bedroom we can see an angular, elderly lady who is seated at a typewriter on which she slowly clicks. In the window seat a young girl of about thirteen dressed in a short cotton frock is reading a book. She is an incredibly thin, solemn, untidy little girl with short, tangled fair hair and bright, intelligent eyes.*]

SERVANT: Well, about Mrs Mulpeter. Did I tell you about Mrs Mulpeter, the poor lamb? [*She goes to the sideboard and then returns.*] Ttt-ttt-ttt. Three days she's been now and three long nights. Think of that now, isn't it a shocking, oh, a shocking thing! [*She works vigorously for a time.*] Such a time as we've had. God knows it's a terrible thing to be a woman. [*There is a knock at the door.*] That was a knock at the door. [*But she pays no attention to it.*] If some of them fellows could be made to suffer half what a woman has to put up with! Oh, my blood boils whenever I think of poor Mrs Mulpeter lying there in pain. Ttt-ttt-ttt.

[*She goes out. The click of the typewriter, which had stopped during her remarks, recommences and continues until her return with the tray.*]

Well, I censed the room a bit then, and I gave her a spoonful of holy water. Take this, Mrs Mulpeter, says I, take this between your poor lips and it will be like a novena to the blessed St Margaret, the friend of all women in your condition. [*The knock is repeated louder.*] There's that knock again. Maybe there's someone at the door. [*She goes as if to open it, but stops on the way.*] Isn't it a terrible thing for me to be quietly laying the supper-table here as if there was no trouble in the world to torture and torment a decent woman! I think I'll go across now and see her, supper or no supper.

[*She goes out again and the typewriter recommences. The girl peers out the window. Presently the* SERVANT *comes back with her hat and coat on.*]

SERVANT: Yes, I'm off now, supper or no supper, and you can tell them that with my compliments.

[*The knock is repeated still louder. The girl draws the curtains about her. The* SERVANT *goes to the hall door and flings it open.*]

Now, now, what's all this? What's going on here?

VISITOR: Excuse.

SERVANT: Are you the ignorant bosthoon that's banging and hammering away at my knocker?

[*Upon the threshold is a pleasant-faced gentleman whose clothes suggest his continental origin. He has close-cut, greyish-fair hair and steady blue eyes. He is in the early forties, and a general air of physical well-being is set off by the punctilious charm of his manner. He has a scar upon one of his cheeks and speaks excellent English with a clipped, meticulous pronunciation, occasionally accenting the wrong syllable and having a little difficulty with his 'th' and his 'w'.*]

VISITOR: Pardon, I hope that I have not inconvenienced the Herr Doktor?

SERVANT: You ought to know better at your age than to be clattering and thumping on respectable people's hall doors.

VISITOR: But, excuse. I am a visitor. I wish to come in.

SERVANT: I don't care if you're the Lord Mayor of Jerusalem, you'd better learn to conduct yourself. Not to speak of the clattering racket of them mechanicalisms out there driving the blessed sleep from her poor tired eyes.

VISITOR: Perhaps you will kindly take my card.

SERVANT: Oh it's little I can do to ease you in your trouble, poor Mrs Mulpeter, little and all.

VISITOR: Pardon?

SERVANT: Ttt-ttt-ttt! Shocking, shocking!

[*She goes out, leaving the door open. He stares after her in some bewilderment. He peers into the room and slowly enters.*]

VISITOR: Herr Doktor.

[*A sudden click of the typewriter makes him start. Finally he*

goes across and proceeds to examine the toy railway in a ten-
tative manner. The GIRL *emerges from behind the curtain and*
approaches him silently.]

GIRL: Nobody's allowed to touch that.

VISITOR [*with a start*]: *Himmel!*

GIRL: What does that mean?

VISITOR: It means, my dear young lady, that you gave me a
surprise.

GIRL: I suppose you don't know who I am?

VISITOR: I am afraid not. But they say that Beauty is a good
letter of introduction, eh?

GIRL: I thought you wouldn't know me, but I know you.
You're the man from the Power House. Sometimes I look
in through the windows and see you working.

VISITOR: So? You do?

GIRL: Hh-hh!

VISITOR: I will certainly look out for you to-morrow.

GIRL: You're a German, aren't you?

VISITOR: That is so, indeed.

GIRL: I was born in Germany.

VISITOR: Ach! Then we are compatriots. You are perhaps the
daughter of the Herr Doktor?

GIRL [*nods*]: At least it was somewhere out there. I'm not very
good at geography. Perhaps you know a place called
Bratislav?

VISITOR: I know the place well. I have passed by in the boats
many times on the trip to Budapest. So that is where you
were born!

GIRL: Well, there's a convent near there. Father was doing
something to a bridge at the time, but of course I was too
young to remember. I say, aren't you going to sit down?

VISITOR: *Bitte sehr.* But, as you say, Ladies first!

GIRL: Oh, I'm not a lady.

VISITOR: *Nicht wahr!* but a very charming one.

GIRL: I'm afraid not. But it's my father's fault. He calls me a little slut, but I think it's calling people things that makes them it, don't you? Oh, what's that little thing on the back of your hat?

VISITOR: This? Oh, it is nothing. We wear them so at home.

GIRL: It's awfully funny. [*She takes his hat.*] Just like a little brush – Oh, it comes in and out!

VISITOR: *Nein – Nein!* It – *Ach*, yes. I see now that it comes in and out.

GIRL: Isn't it meant to? I haven't broken it?

VISITOR: Not at all, my dear young lady. It is quite all right.

GIRL: I'm afraid I *have* broken it. You're not telling me the truth.

VISITOR: Please do not bother. *Das macht nichts.*

GIRL: Can you mend it?

VISITOR: I can procure another. It is nothing.

GIRL: I'm rather unlucky with things, but it's not really my fault, you know. At least, hardly ever. They always say it is, though.

VISITOR: One's parents never do understand, do they?

GIRL: I haven't any parents.

VISITOR: No parents – ? But –

GIRL: Not unless you count father.

VISITOR: One usually counts one's father.

GIRL: Not ones like mine. We don't get on very well, I'm afraid. I can't remember my mother.

VISITOR: So.

GIRL: But there's a picture of her out in the Armoury. She has fair hair and the loveliest hands. I think she's pretty, but we don't know much about her. Except father, and of course he says nothing. Have you got any parents?

VISITOR: No, I am afraid not.

GIRL: Then, I suppose we're both orphans in a sense. But I daresay you've been better brought up than me?

VISITOR [*laughing*]: Well, that is a very difficult question. What would you say was being – well brought up?

GIRL: Oh, going to a proper school instead of being taught by Auntie and George. That's Auntie typing up there. She knows Medieval History and Latin, and George knows a lot of awfully good Sea Shanties. But you can't go far on that, can you? Nowadays, I mean.

VISITOR: Well, it all depends upon what you want.

GIRL: I think that every girl needs an education nowadays in order to prepare her for the battle of life. She wants to be taught Deportment and Geography and Religious Knowledge and – oh – Mathematics. I adore Mathematics, don't you?

VISITOR: *Ach*, but you are the daughter of a great engineer. Most young ladies of my acquaintance try to avoid these things and to stay away from school.

GIRL: Perhaps that's because they have got more suitable parents. My father says that education poisons the mind, but I say he was educated himself, so his mind must be poisoned, and if it's poisoned, how can he know what's good for me?

VISITOR: And what has he got to say to that?

GIRL: Nothing. He just looks at me – the way he always does. I don't know why. Don't you think it must be wonderful to have proper lessons and sleep in an enormous dormitory with twenty other girls and go for walks in a long line like geese? Tell me, have you ever looked through a convent keyhole?

VISITOR: *Ach!* No – I have not had that experience!

GIRL: Well, you can see them in there. Walking about in the garden, always in threes – never in pairs. That's how I know all about it. I wish you would take a look some day. Then you might be able to tell me whether you think they're very much more advanced than I am.

VISITOR: But you have no other young friends?

GIRL: No. There isn't anybody much out here except the men going out on the wall to the lighthouse. I think that Darry Blake is my only real friend. Do you know him?

VISITOR: No.

GIRL: He used to come across the bay a lot when he had the waterwag, and sometimes he'd take me up to the pictures. But he hardly ever comes now. I think he must have dropped us. We're not awfully good, you know – socially, I mean.

VISITOR: I am sure that it cannot be that. But perhaps, when we are better acquainted, I may be permitted to take you up to the pictures instead.

GIRL: Oh, would you? How lovely! When? To-morrow?

VISITOR: I would be charmed. But first we must ask the permission of your distinguished father.

GIRL: Oh, he won't care.

VISITOR: *Ach*, but you see, I do not know the Herr Doktor very well. This is the first occasion on which I have had the honour of his invitation to supper.

GIRL: Oh, supper! Is that why you called?

VISITOR: Then, you do not expect me?

GIRL: Oh, I'm sure it's all right. People do sometimes come to supper. Perhaps I'd better go and tell father.

VISITOR: You are very kind. But if I am not expected – !

GIRL: Oh, I wouldn't mind that. [*Turning at the bottom of the stairs*]: I think you were wonderful about the pictures. I do hope you're not annoyed about that little thing I broke?

VISITOR [*distressed*]: Not at all, I assure you. Perhaps it would be well for me to call another time.

GIRL: I didn't think you would be annoyed, really. But don't tell father, please. He'd only say it was what he expected of me or something. I'll get him now.

[*She goes upstairs. He takes a step after her, but decides to wait, and sits down uncomfortably in a big chair with his back to the stairs.*]

AUNT [*from her room*]: Blanaid!

GIRL: Yes?

AUNT: Who's that?

BLANAID: The man from the Power House.

AUNT: What does he want?

BLANAID: He wants to stay to supper, and for me to come to the pictures to-morrow.

AUNT: Was he asked?

BLANAID: He says so.

AUNT: I don't believe it for a minute.

BLANAID: Hush, Auntie! He's listening.

AUNT: Well, listeners never hear any good of themselves.

BLANAID: I'm supposed to tell father.

AUNT: Well, if he stays, I go.

BLANAID: Ss-sssh! [*with a glance at the speechless Foreigner*]: It's all right. I don't think he heard.

[*She goes off down the gallery. Presently the* AUNT *emerges from her bedroom and comes quietly downstairs. She is a lean and vigorous woman of about fifty, with bright fanatical eyes. She wears a tweed skirt and a Fair Isle sweater that comes to her throat. Her hair, once very beautiful and still uncut, is now streaked with grey and is untidily done. She comes to the table in the centre and removes a silver flower vase which, with a look of deep suspicion at the* VISITOR, *she brings back to her room. She is almost at the table before he notices her and springs to his feet bowing politely. After she has gone he decides to steal away, but before he has got as far as the open hall door, there is a sound of voices from outside and two men enter. They are* GEORGE *and his friend and crony,* CAPT. POTTS. *They are both well-seasoned and weather-beaten salts – the former a tall, lean man with brown wrinkled skin, dressed in a loose-fitting double-breasted grey tweed suit. He still has the face and carriage of an incurable romanticist, which he has never ceased to be since he ran away to sea from a comfortable home and a good family fifty years ago. Since then he has been all over the world, fought in half a dozen campaigns, and come through them all unscathed both in mind and in body. The only regular feature in his life has been its unvarying lack of money, for on the occasions on which he has managed to acquire any, he has always lost it promptly, thanks to his uneconomic enthusiasms and his impulsive habit of backing bills for insolvent friends. For the last seven of his ripening years he has more or less settled down in a Government appointment that takes him about the coast, drilling crews and inspecting the life-saving apparatus. His old friend, CAPT. POTTS, is storekeeper. The latter, a fat old Cockney, with a heavy grey moustache, is dressed in his best blue serge with collar and tie, and a sailor's cap and has a black crêpe band on his sleeve. He carries a large bunch of flowers. Neither of them at first takes any notice of the Foreigner.]*

GEORGE and POTTS [*singing off*]:
Oh, whiskey is the life of man,
O whiskey Johnny!
I'll drink whiskey when I can,
O whiskey for my Johnny.

O whiskey makes you feel so gran',
O whiskey Johnny!
Whiskey from an old tin can,
O whiskey for my Johnny!

GEORGE [*as he enters*]: Bring 'em in, Potts, bring 'em in. Don't be shy, old man, there's nobody here. We'll get something for them over here. [*He goes to a cupboard and selects a glass jar.*] Perhaps we'd better put some water in it.
POTTS: Ri. [*To VISITOR.*] Bettter for a drop o' water, y' know.
GEORGE [*filling the jar from the carafe on the table*]: There now, shove 'em into that, old man. Much too late, don't you think?
POTTS: Sure, Gent 'ere, George.
GEORGE: What's that? Who? Why, so there is, b' Gad. Friend of yours, Potts?
POTTS: Nope.

GEORGE [*as they carefully arrange the flowers*]: Suppose we'd better have a word with the fellow. No good in being stand-offish, eh?

POTTS: Just as you say, George.

GEORGE: Well, what do you think of that little lot?

VISITOR: Very nice, I am sure.

GEORGE: Meet my friend Capt. Potts. In charge of my store.

VISITOR: I am delighted to meet you, Herr Kapitän.

POTTS: 'At's aw ri'.

GEORGE: You're the fellow from the Power House. I know you. Like to shake hands?

VISITOR: With pleasure.

GEORGE: Gooden tag! Shake hands with Potts, too. Shake hands with him, Potts, old man. These fellows love shaking hands.

[POTTS *does.*]

POTTS: Gooden tag. [*Laughter.*]

VISITOR: I know you and your friend by sight. You manage the rocket apparatus. You save lives from the ships in distress, eh?

GEORGE: That's right. Do you like these flowers? [*Whispering*]: Say you do. For the old man.

VISITOR: You are fond of flowers?

GEORGE: They're not for himself, you know. [*Whispering*]: His wife's dead.

VISITOR: *Ach*, I am so sorry! A recent demise?

GEORGE: About sixteen years. Sixteen – is that right, Potts?

POTTS: Sixteen, eggsackly.

GEORGE: Very sad for the poor old fellow.

VISITOR [*rather at a loss*]: Oh – Yes. Er, I like your flowers, Herr Kapitän.

POTTS: Think they'll do?

VISITOR: *Sehr schön*.

GEORGE: Say you like his suit, too. Only puts it on once a year. Wife's anniversary. It was her favourite suit. Poor old

Potts. [*He sniffs.*] I wonder is there anything in here. [*He inspects the cupboard again and produces a whiskey bottle.*] How about it, Potts, old man? Drink, Herr Splosch?

VISITOR: Tausch is my name.

POTTS: Ri'. I'll 'ave a small 'un.

GEORGE: You'll have to share a glass with Potts, I'm afraid. Mind sharing a glass with Herr Splosch, Potts?

POTTS: Naw. 'Salls same.

TAUSCH: I thank you, but I do not take spirits.

GEORGE: What? No spirits.

TAUSCH: No, thank you.

GEORGE: Really?

TAUSCH: Unfortunately they do not agree with me.

GEORGE: Most extraordinary! Well, you know yourself best. There you are, old man.

POTTS: 'At'll do.

GEORGE: Pour it down, Potts.

POTTS: Well – 'ere's looking at yer.

GEORGE: We got as far as the Scotch House, you know. But I said to Capt. Potts here, 'Potts, it's all very well, old man, but I think we've started too late. Take a taxi and we'll have no damn money to get home. Take a tram and the damn cemetery'll be closed by the time we get there. It's no good bringing flowers to a cemetery when it's closed, is it?'

TAUSCH: You bring these flowers to the tomb?

GEORGE: Yes, you know the poor old fellow's wife's dead. Anniversary. We always go.

POTTS: Yes, mush too late.

GEORGE: So when we left the Scotch House, I said, 'Come on back to the store, Capt. Potts, and we'll put those flowers in water and try again to-morrow.'

POTTS: 'Ave to go again.

TAUSCH: The Scotch House is closed to-morrow, I suppose?

GEORGE: Oh no, Sunday. Different hours, that's all. Well, when we saw the door open on our way back, we thought we'd come in to look for some water. And, by God, we got it, eh, Potts old man?

POTTS [*refreshed*]: You betcher life!

GEORGE: Good thing we came in, Potts, or we wouldn't have met Herr Splosch. Are you sure now you won't have a small one?

TAUSCH: No, thank you.

GEORGE: Well, you must step across to the store some time and we'll give you a rosner. You know – just next door in the old Armoury.

TAUSCH: I think that I know the place.

GEORGE: Everybody welcome. Just like in this house. Eh, Potts?

POTTS: Liberty 'All.

GEORGE [*singing*]: 'Sally Brown, she's a bright Mullatter.'

BOTH: 'Way – ay – y, roll and go.'

GEORGE: 'She drinks rum and chews tobacker.'

BOTH: 'Spend my money on Sally Brown.'

GEORGE: 'Sally Brown, she has a daughter.'

BOTH: 'Way – ay – y, roll and go.'

GEORGE: 'Sent me sailing across the water.'

POTTS: 'Spend my money on Sally Br—'

GEORGE: Steady, Potts old man, steady. Can't make a row in other people's houses, you know.

POTTS [*abashed*]: 'At's ri', George. Shouldn't do that.

GEORGE [*mysteriously*]: Listen! You're a foreigner. Do you know anything about guns?

TAUSCH: Guns?

GEORGE: Don't mention it much. But come along some time and I'll show you something will surprise you.

[*The* HOST *and his* DAUGHTER *appear at the top of the stairs. He is a distinguished-looking elderly gentleman with a refined sensitive face and the delicate nervous hands of an artist. There is a certain ruthlessness – one would almost say, cruelty – about his fastidious lips and chin that seems to be*

*perpetually at war with his eyes, which are imaginative and
sympathetic. He dresses carelessly in tweeds, but with good
taste, and his manner betokens an inborn restlessness. He
comes down the stairs quickly, his hand outstretched.*]

HOST: Why, my dear sir, I had no idea that you were here.
You must accept my sincerest apologies. Put on the light,
Blanaid.

TAUSCH: Good evening, Mr Dobelle. I am afraid that I have
called unawares.

DOBELLE: Not at all, not at all. I was buried in the library,
and nobody dreamt of telling me you were here. Deuced
unmannerly house this.

TAUSCH: *Im Gegenteil.* I have been entertained most charm-
ingly by your daughter.

[BLANAID *from the stairs flings him a smile, points to her
head and places a finger to her lips.*]

GEORGE: We thought you'd like us to give him a drink. So
we did.

DOBELLE: Well, thank God for that! I hope there was
enough.

[*He lifts the empty decanter and looks at* TAUSCH *in some
surprise.*]

GEORGE: Oh yes, lots, old man, lots.

DOBELLE: You have met George, then?

TAUSCH: We have introduced ourselves. Oh, I assure you, I
have – how you say – I have been done proud.

DOBELLE: Let me take your coat.

TAUSCH: Believe me, sir, since first I came to reside at the
Power House, I have been looking forward to the pleasure
of this visit.

DOBELLE: Very handsome of you to say so, I'm sure. We
haven't much to offer, I'm afraid.

BLANAID: You can't stay to supper, George. There's
only just enough as it is, and Agnes has gone off somewhere.

GEORGE: That's all right, my dear. We're not staying. Only dropped in to entertain Herr Splosch. Come along, Potts, old man.

POTTS: Well – By –

GEORGE: So long, everyone.

TAUSCH: *Auf Wiedersehen.*

GEORGE: *Auf Wiedersehen?* Did you hear that, Potts? That was German. And don't forget what I told you. Any time you're passing. Like to show you what I mentioned. *Wiedersehen!* Ha-ha! Ha-ha! Damned silly language. Ha-ha-ha!

[*They go and are heard singing off for a moment,* POTTS *after a moment's hesitation in the door coming back for his flowers and removing them vase and all.*]

DOBELLE: Do sit down, sir.

TAUSCH: With pleasure.

DOBELLE: I'm very glad George gave you a drink. He's a dear fellow, but rather a rolling stone. Very good company out here where company is scarce.

TAUSCH: It is farther from the town than I had imagined. This place is very old?

DOBELLE: No, just a relic of the Napoleon scare. Derelict for about fifty years before I took it for my hermitage. Darrell Blake could tell you all about its history.

TAUSCH: I do not think that I have met him. But your daughter mentioned his name.

DOBELLE: He's one of our few regular visitors. But lately he's got a little involved in other things and we don't see him so often. It is a pity. I find, Herr Tausch, that there are very few people in this world that are at all tolerable to talk to.

TAUSCH: I respectfully agree. That is why I feel so honoured in being invited to share your hospitality, Mr Dobelle. You – a distinguished railway engineer – I have so often in my student days read your articles in the technical journals.

Little did I think that one day I would have you as my neighbour.

DOBELLE: Tut, tut. No man should be reminded of the articles that he has written.

TAUSCH: When first I decided to come to this part of the world my friends they all say: 'But why do you wish to go there?' I answer, 'Ha-ha, I know what I am doing.' And now I write home and I say, 'I told you so. I am the neighbour of the man whose works I have studied for so many years – Mr Dobelle.'

DOBELLE: Still, that scarcely answers their question, does it? Why should you wish to come here?

TAUSCH: *Ach*, how can one say. It is the call of the West Wind. One grows tired of those places where everything has been done already. Then one day comes the call of Romance. I answer. You understand.

DOBELLE: I certainly do not. It sounds like nonsense to me.

TAUSCH: *Ach*, but I cannot believe that. You wish me to believe that you smile at sentiment, but that is only a charming conceit, if I may say so. I know that you can appreciate the charm of the West, Mr Dobelle, and, believe me, I had spent but a very few weeks upon my course before I realized how right I had been.

DOBELLE: Oh, you took a course?

TAUSCH: But naturally. When one goes to live in a strange land, is it too much that one should try to acquaint oneself with the customs of the people?

DOBELLE: We have some customs here that I fancy it would be difficult to understand in München. But be specific now and tell me frankly what is there here that can possibly interest an intelligent hydro-electrical engineer?

TAUSCH: Might I not put that question to yourself, Mr Dobelle? You seem to find something to interest you.

DOBELLE: My wander-years are over. I have come home to renounce them.

TAUSCH: Precisely. You have travelled the world and have
come to the conclusion that your own place is the best after all.

DOBELLE: No. I doubt if I could explain to you, Herr Tausch.
It's a purely personal point of view. But I find that the
world you speak of maddens me.

TAUSCH: I think I understand. You prefer the life of the
spirit. You long for – how does it go? –

'. . . magic casements opening on the foam
Of perilous seas in faery lands forlorn.'

DOBELLE: Ridiculous. Nobody but a Cockney could have
conjured up such a picture. Don't be deceived, Herr
Tausch. Here by the waters of Lethe we may believe in
fairies, but we trade in pigs. No. I think it was those very
pigs that called me back. It takes one a long time to find
one's spiritual home, but revelation comes at last, my friend.
Isn't it Goethe who tells us that when we are old we must
do more than when we are young? Don't believe a word of
it, my dear sir. Once I served Righteousness with that in-
tense desire for service that one has in one's youth. I studied
hard, read everything that came my way, and built railway
bridges anywhere from Hungary to the Gran Chaco. But
since my revelation I amuse myself with toy trains instead
of real ones and read little else but the *Encyclopaedia*. And
believe me, I find it much more satisfactory.

TAUSCH [*smiling*]: I suspect, Mr Dobelle, that you visited
China as well as the Gran Chaco.

DOBELLE: I suppose every cock crows loudest on its own
dunghill. Here it is still possible to live on one's own mind.
Even if usually it proves a mighty poor diet. And speaking
of diet, I did ask you to supper, didn't I?

TAUSCH: If it inconveniences you in any way –

DOBELLE: No, no; he who works may eat. Agnes! I wonder
where Agnes is?

[*The* AUNT *appears at the top of the stairs. She has put on
her hat and coat.*]

AUNT: Agnes has gone. [*She goes away again.*]

DOBELLE: Gone! Damnation!

BLANAID: It's all right. The table's nearly laid. Mrs Mulpeter is going to have a baby.

DOBELLE: What, again? I never heard of such a thing!

BLANAID: The supper is on the range. [*To* TAUSCH]: Do you mind finishing the table while I go and get it?

TAUSCH: *Ja gewiss.* With pleasure.

DOBELLE [*making no effort to help*]: This is too bad! too bad! Leaving the table half laid! And the supper on the range! Without as much as with your leave or by your leave!

TAUSCH: It is a privilege, I assure you. I enjoy the helping very much indeed.

DOBELLE: Servants are insufferable. Why can't we do without them? [*The* AUNT *appears again at the top of the stairs carrying a bicycle which she brings down with her.*] What the devil has happened to supper? I ask Herr Tausch here to supper. I give notice to you all. He comes. There is nothing to eat and he has to lay the table himself. Don't answer me back.

AUNT: Who cares about supper! Maybe there'll be more than supper to bother about by the time this night is out.

DOBELLE: A nice way to treat a guest. Oh, Herr Tausch, may I introduce my sister, Columba.

TAUSCH [*bowing*]: *Gnädige Frau.* I think that we have met already to-night.

AUNT: I daresay you expect me to shake hands with you; but even if I would, I can't with this bicycle.

TAUSCH: Perhaps you will allow me to assist you with it.

AUNT: Leave it alone, please. I know how to look after my own bicycle.

TAUSCH: I am so sorry.

DOBELLE: She doesn't like people to touch her things, Tausch. That's why she keeps it in her bedroom.

TAUSCH: I see.

AUNT: And take my advice, my good man, don't leave any of your property round here if you ever want to see it again. A word to the wise.

DOBELLE: Columba, you're not going out before supper?

AUNT: I am. I have work to do. Sometimes there are too many strangers in this house.

DOBELLE: Oh well, have it your own way. Better let her go, Tausch, if she wants to.

TAUSCH: My dear sir, I had no intention of interfering with her departure.

AUNT: I'd just like to see you try. [*She pauses at the door and feels in her pocket.*] You'd better take one of these. They'll all be gone when I get back. [*She hands him a typewritten pamphlet.*]

TAUSCH: *Danke sehr.*

AUNT: I daresay the turbines are humming merrily now. The dynamos are turning and the water piles up behind the sluices. You think you have done well. But you haven't accounted for everything. No, you haven't accounted for everything, my good man.

[*The* AUNT *goes.* BLANAID *enters with a tray.*]

TAUSCH: *Grüss Gott.*

BLANAID: Supper!

DOBELLE: At last. Sit down, Tausch, and let us atone for our laxity with a bottle of hock. Where's the corkscrew? [*He takes a bottle from the cupboard.*]

TAUSCH [*reading*]: 'Our existence is not the aftermath of a past revolt. It is the presage of a future one. We shall rise again.'

DOBELLE: What's that? Where's the corkscrew?

TAUSCH: 'We shall rise again.' What is this?

DOBELLE: Oh, that? Just propaganda. She types them herself and pastes them up on the tram posts in town.

TAUSCH: *Ach, fliegende Blätter.* Politics.

DOBELLE: Here's the corkscrew. Yes, she's been in jail once or twice. You mustn't mind it.

TAUSCH: In jail? So interesting.

DOBELLE [*drawing the cork*]: Oh yes. In and out. But she's not typical of the country.

TAUSCH: I do not think that I have met many people who have been often in jail.

DOBELLE: It's one of the best qualifications for a public appointment. Hock?

TAUSCH: With pleasure.

DOBELLE [*filling his glass*]: I always say it's a pity she never got married; but her only serious affair ended in rather a row. Something about a mowing machine. And, by the way, while I remember, better not mention the matter to her. She's rather sensitive.

TAUSCH [*drawing another typewritten document from his pocket*]: My dear sir, I would not think of doing so. But I wonder does what you tell me throw any light upon a strange communication which I received a few days ago?

DOBELLE: Let me see. [*He takes it.*] Oh-ho! A threat to the works! You got this a day or two ago?

TAUSCH: Yes. One of my men found it pinned to the door of the Switch House.

DOBELLE: Were you at all put out by this?

TAUSCH: I did not understand it, my dear sir. Some people object because I supply power and light to the Military Barracks. I did not think it of much consequence, because when I notify the Police they say that it will be quite all right. I am more than relieved to learn that it may only be your charming sister.

DOBELLE: I wonder. The situation is a little different from what you are accustomed to. In most countries the political idealist is merely a bore. But here he has a disconcerting tradition of action. He usually has his own Government and his own Army as well, you see.

TAUSCH: You mean to say that he does not recognize the machinery of democracy?

DOBELLE: He would say that you don't understand democracy. The Will of the People is a tender delicate bloom to
be nurtured by the elect few who know best. The icy blasts
of a general election are not for it. There's some sense in
it – when you know that you know best.

TAUSCH: That is a little metaphysical for me.

DOBELLE: Metaphysical? My dear fellow, it's simply Christian Science applied to politics. If you don't like the Government you deny its existence – a state of affairs which is
sometimes a little embarrassing for the likes of you and me.

BLANAID: Willie's out to-night. I saw him go off with his
whistle and his water-bottle.

DOBELLE: Oh? I suppose it's useless to say anything to
Darrell.

TAUSCH: And your other acquaintance – the gentleman
whose friend has suffered the so sad bereavement – would
he be one of these too?

DOBELLE: Who? George? Well, not really. He's a barbarian,
but an amiable one. When did Willie go off?

BLANAID: About half past six.

DOBELLE: Oh well, there's nothing can be done now. A little
more hock, Tausch?

TAUSCH: With pleasure. And what will you have, young
lady?

BLANAID [taking the carafe]: Only this, thanks.

TAUSCH: 'And Roman women were of old for drink content
with water.' Eh?

DOBELLE: Prosit. [They rise.]

TAUSCH: Prosit.
    [They drink.]
    Go muh shocht noora nees farr hoo bleeun oh nyoo.

DOBELLE [after a surprised pause]: Part of your course, no
doubt?

BLANAID: That's Irish. He was only trying to say, 'May you
feel better next year.'

TAUSCH: And this is the little Miss who pretends to have no education!

[DOBELLE *looks at her silently for a moment and then sits down.*]

DOBELLE: I suppose that's what Columba teaches you. Well, after this display of erudition, perhaps we may get on with supper.

[AGNES *enters by the hall door.*]

AGNES: Tt–ttt–tt–tt.

DOBELLE: So here you are!

AGNES: Yes, here I am. I thought I'd come back for a short bit. But she's very bad.

DOBELLE: I'm afraid there's not much more for you to do.

AGNES: That's just as well. They may want me back any minute. They've sent for the doctor. So I propped her up on the pillows and I wrapped a vinegared handkerchief round her poor head. 'Poor Mrs Mulpeter,' says I, 'isn't that nyummy nyumm? God help you, it won't be long now.' And neither it will. I'd be ashamed and me a man to be quietly eating supper and drinking strong drink and poor Mrs Mulpeter so near to her great trouble. [*She goes into the kitchen.*]

DOBELLE: Well, I suppose we must be thankful for small mercies.

TAUSCH: I understand. A lady is in childbirth. It is a very trying time. Yes. One can excuse a lot at such moments. I remember when my dear wife was –

AGNES [*putting her head in the door*]: Now, now; none of that! I'll have none of that sort of talk while I'm about, if you please. Think shame to you – a couple of men to be gostering and making chatter about the trouble and misfortune tormenting a poor woman.

TAUSCH: Pardon.

[*They eat in silence for a few minutes.* AGNES *enters again.*]

AGNES [*putting a plate on the table*]: I made them move her downstairs, so I did. In the top room of the gate-house she

B

was. But I said No. That child must not be carried downstairs until it's carried upstairs first or I'll know the reason
why, and if the poor mite starts at the top of the house, how
can it go upstairs first? So down to the sitting-room poor
Mrs Mulpeter had to come. The agony the poor creature
suffered! Tt-tt-tt – [*She goes.*]

DOBELLE: Oh, by the way, Tausch, I should have mentioned
it before, but do be careful what you say in front of Agnes.
She's very puritanical. You understand?

TAUSCH: I will try to remember that too.

DOBELLE: We find it best to attune our conversation to the
tastes of our servants. Let's go back to George. He's quite
a non-committal subject. Have a sausage? George, you
know, is the best of fellows. Calls himself a Christian Com-
munist and wants everybody to be free and happy and at
peace. But every time that the people try to be free and
happy and peaceful it seems to George that somebody
comes along and stops them with big guns.

TAUSCH: So?

DOBELLE: Well, a few years ago, George, the most practical
of men, decided to make a big gun for himself, so that the
next time the people won't be so badly off. He's been at it
on and off ever since.

TAUSCH: To *make* a big gun?

DOBELLE: Exactly. And with quite surprising results. Of
course nobody knows what will happen when it's fired.
But we all hope for the best. Naturally, this is all in the
strictest confidence. You must get him to show it to you the
next time you're passing the Armoury.

TAUSCH: I certainly will. But what industry! What en-
thusiasm!

DOBELLE: And why not, if one believes as George does? If
you, Herr Tausch, a complete stranger, can come here to
harness our tides for us, why be surprised when George
tries to do something for the country too?

TAUSCH: But, my dear sir – to make a big gun! It is a year's work!

DOBELLE: About four years, as a matter of fact. And about a year extra for each projectile. Yes, they started on the fourth shell in the spring.

TAUSCH: Colossal!

DOBELLE: Oh yes, in about twenty years' time we'll be getting quite formidable.

TAUSCH: Ah now, sir, I am afraid you are jesting. Of course it is not the application that I admire. I am not so materialistic. But the Spirit – the Praxis – it is an example. Please excuse while I make a note in my book for my next letter to my son Karl.

DOBELLE: Well, well, I'm sure George would be delighted to know that he had been a help to Karl. You have a large family?

TAUSCH: Not very large. Four children only. They are still young and at school. That is why I have to leave them behind when I come here.

DOBELLE: You must miss them all.

TAUSCH: I confess that sometimes I do. In the evenings especially I miss the music.

DOBELLE: You are fond of music?

TAUSCH: But naturally. We all love music in Bavaria. You are musical, too, perhaps?

DOBELLE: Oh, very.

TAUSCH: What instruments do you play?

DOBELLE: None, I'm afraid.

BLANAID: We had a piano once, but it got stuck.

TAUSCH: Stuck?

BLANAID: Yes. It's out in the Armoury now.

TAUSCH: The sea air, I suppose?

DOBELLE: You play yourself, of course?

TAUSCH: Oh yes. We all play. I play the cello and my dear wife she plays very beautifully upon the piano. My daughter – the eldest one, Lotte – she is the violinist of the family.

DOBELLE: Quite a little orchestra, in fact.

TAUSCH: Oh, that is not all. Karl, my first son, he plays the viola, and Hermann, the second boy, plays the flute. And even my little Greta – she is only five years – we are teaching her to accompany us upon the triangle.

DOBELLE: Charming.

TAUSCH: We were to buy an electric organ when I decided to come away. Just a small organ, but a beautiful instrument. However, we found that the vibration would be dangerous for a wooden house. So this winter they are laying down a concrete foundation and that will make it all right, I think.

DOBELLE: A concrete foundation? For the organ, you mean?

TAUSCH: Yes.

BLANAID: Oh, how lovely!

TAUSCH: Each evening in my room at the Works I play to myself when I can afford the time, just to keep in practice. I am afraid you will think me a little sentimental. But the melodies that we are fond of, what else can bring back to us in the same way the mountains, the lakes, the wife and children that one loves? You understand.

DOBELLE [humming]:
   Kennst du das Land, wo die Zitronen blühn?
   Im dunkeln Laub die Gold-Orangen glühn.

TAUSCH:
   Ein sanfter Wind vom blauen Himmel weht.
   Die Myrte still und hoch der Lorbeer steht –
   Kennst du es wohl?
         Dahin! Dahin!
   Möcht ich mit dir, o mein Geliebter, ziehn.

DOBELLE [after a pause]: You know, I feel distinct pathos when you sing that song.

TAUSCH: Ah, Mr Dobelle, I am so glad to have met you here.

I feel that I will find in you a friend, not of my fortune, but of myself. Yes, I am truly happy to know you.

DOBELLE: I don't think you should ever have come here. I shudder to think what is before you.

TAUSCH: I only hope that I may be able to help you. I love your country and would serve it even in some small way.

DOBELLE: Yes, that is what I feared, and I know that I should resent it, but I haven't the heart. You are in higher hands. Still, I can't help being sorry for you.

TAUSCH: Sorry for me? May I ask why?

DOBELLE: Because, Herr Tausch, I like you, and at the same time I see with infinite pathos the not far distant date when, if you stay here, you will find yourself out. And that to my mind is always a pity.

TAUSCH: I do not understand.

DOBELLE: It is not the destiny of a man like you to be buried in this accursed hole. Take my tip before it is too late. Leave your Power House and go.

TAUSCH: Leave my Power House? What joke is this?

DOBELLE: Have you ever heard of the Bogy Man, Herr Tausch? Well, here we have Bogy Men, fierce and terrible Bogy Men, who breathe fire from their nostrils and vanish in the smoke.

TAUSCH: You have what?

DOBELLE: And we have vampires in shimmering black that feed on blood and bear bombs instead of brats. And enormous fat crows that will never rest until they have pecked out your eyes and left you blind and dumb with terror.

TAUSCH: Come, come, Mr Dobelle.

DOBELLE: And in the mists that creep down from the mountains you will meet monsters that glare back at you with your own face.

TAUSCH: Ah now, Mr Dobelle, you cannot frighten me with parables. You forget that I am a German, and what you say only convinces me how much you really need my work.

DOBELLE: I know that nobody will ever listen to me; but, remember, I have warned you.

TAUSCH: I think, if I may say so, that you are a little afraid of life and that is why you live here. But we are not like that in Germany. There we still have the virile youth of a new nation: hope, courage, and the ability to rise again. Put Germany in the saddle and you will find that she can ride. Just a little organization here and you will see the change. Do not please think that I am preaching the doctrines of material prosperity. That matters nothing. [*The sound of a motor-car comes from outside and headlamps throw a beam of light on the blinds of the window.*] It is here, in the brain, that we find all that is of any value. It is the change of Mind that only Power can bring that will be the justification for all my work here. As Schiller tells us, Freedom cannot exist save when united with Might. And what Might can equal electrical power at one farthing a unit? [*On the blinds appears the shadow of a man in an overcoat holding something in his hand that closely resembles a revolver.*] I see in my mind's eye this land of the future – transformed and redeemed by Power – from the sordid trivialities of peasant life to something newer and better. Soon you will be a happy nation of free men – free not by the magic of empty formulae or by the colour of the coats you wear, but by the inspiration of Power – Power – Power. And in that day I shall say in the words of Horace ...

[*He notices the silence of the other two and follows their eyes to the window. Presently a* GUNMAN *enters silently through the door. He wears a waterproof coat and a soft cap and the lower part of his face is masked by a handkerchief. He carries a revolver. The two men sit in silence, the* HOST *limply, the* VISITOR *rigid. Then the older man eats a piece of bread.*]

GUNMAN: All the men in this house will have to be searched for arms.

[*Silence.* BLANAID *at last rises and runs out. For a terrible moment it looks as though she may be shot.*]

GUNMAN: Have you any arms or ammunition?

[*Silence. The* GERMAN *makes a move, but the other with a quick movement restrains him.*]

GUNMAN: Come on, now.

DOBELLE: Now, we're not going to have any shooting here, are we?

GUNMAN: Oh, I'm not so sure of that.

DOBELLE: Well, perhaps you'd better come back another time. When supper's over, maybe, or when I haven't any visitors.

GUNMAN: I'm sorry. I have my orders – from Battalion Headquarters. I have my duty to do.

DOBELLE [*standing*]: Well. . . .

GUNMAN: The house is surrounded.

DOBELLE: I daresay. [*He rings the bell on the table.*]

GUNMAN: Leave that bell alone.

DOBELLE: Certainly. I just thought that as you have to search the men, you might like to see the women, too.

GUNMAN: I don't want to see the women.

DOBELLE: Very well. You can send them away.

[*There is a pause during which the* GUNMAN *shifts uneasily, and the* COOK *enters.*]

DOBELLE: Oh, Agnes, here's somebody who says he wants to search us all for arms.

GUNMAN [*gruffly*]: Everybody ought to put up their hands.

AGNES: If I put up my hands, it'll be to take you across my knee and give you a good skelping where you least expect it.

DOBELLE: An excellent suggestion.

AGNES: Take that old rag off your face at once, Willie Reilly. And who, may I ask, let you in here with them boots on?

GUNMAN [*sheepishly removing his mask and displaying an honest, pink face*]: Aw, I didn't know you knew me.

AGNES: Do you hear me asking you who let you in here with them dirty boots?

GUNMAN: I have me orders, Ma.

AGNES: Well, you have your orders now, and out you go before I lam you with the flat of my fist.

WILLIE: Ay, easy now, Ma.

DOBELLE: Just a moment, Agnes. It seems that Willie's here on military business, and I think it's scarcely fair to pack him off without hearing what it's all about.

WILLIE: That's right, Mr Dobelle.

AGNES: Military business! Indeed! And what sort of military business gives him the right to come trapesing into my clean living-room with the mud of three counties on his boots, I'd like to know? Military business! Go 'long owa that, ye ignorant yuck, before I military business your backside.

WILLIE: Ay, keep off me, Ma.

DOBELLE: Agnes, please. If you don't mind. There's no use being violent. Personally, I'd like to hear what it's all about.

WILLIE: That's right. Now, violence never did any good, Ma. You know that.

AGNES: Oh, very well, very well. Have it your own way. I've got to be off out of this anyway, and it's no concern of mine if you turn the place into a pigsty. But don't ask me to clean up after you. You can do that for yourselves. [*She goes off with a slam into the kitchen.*]

WILLIE: God looka what can a man do with a mother the like of that, tormenting and disgracing him and he on active service! Looka now, I ask you what harm in God's name is my boots doing?

[*The* GERMAN *rises and mops his brow.*]

DOBELLE: Not much, I'm sure, Willie. Don't mind your mother. I'll put in a word for you if I can, and any mess you make you can sweep up for yourself before you go. [*The* GERMAN *whispers to him.*] Oh yes, and Willie, now that we're talking on a friendlier basis, don't you think that you might put that revolver away?

WILLIE: Ah sure, there's nothing in it. But I'll put it in my pocket if you like, sir.

DOBELLE: That's good. This is Mr Tausch of the Power House. Herr Tausch, Willie Reilly, Agnes's first-born.

TAUSCH: I see – Good day.

WILLIE: How-are-ye?

DOBELLE: Won't you sit down, Willie?

WILLIE: Ah no, I can't, thank you very much, sir. I have to be off in a tick. The boys is all outside.

DOBELLE: And what have the boys got on hand, Willie?

WILLIE: Well, the idea is to blow up the Works.

TAUSCH: *Gott in Himmel!*

WILLIE: You know – the Power House.

TAUSCH: You are going to blow up the Power House!

WILLIE: Yes. D'ye know.

TAUSCH: *Almächtiger Gott!* What is all this?

DOBELLE: Just a moment, Tausch. Perhaps you'd better let me talk to him.

TAUSCH: Perhaps I had better!

DOBELLE: Listen, Willie. Why are you proposing to blow up the Power House?

WILLIE: I'm sure I don't know, sir. Battalion orders, d'ye know.

DOBELLE: He says he's under orders.

TAUSCH [*strides to the window and looks out*]: There are men out there. But this cannot be serious.

DOBELLE: It looks rather like it.

TAUSCH: But it is monstrous! Outrageous! There must be some mistake.

DOBELLE: You realize, Willie, that this is all rather upsetting for Mr Tausch. They are his Works, you know.

WILLIE: Indeed, I'm sure he'd have a right to be a bit put out, and I'm sorry indeed to be fixed the way I am. But I have my orders as a soldier, d'ye know, and I've got to obey orders, sir. But there's no ill will at all.

DOBELLE: I know, Willie, I know. I suppose it can't be helped.

WILLIE: You know that, Mr Tausch, don't you? There's no ill will at all.

TAUSCH: Ill will? What is that? I think I go mad!

WILLIE: We'll do the least damage we can, you may be sure.

DOBELLE: I'm sure of that, Willie. But all this doesn't explain what you want here. These aren't the Works, you know.

WILLIE: Well, sir, the fact is the stuff we have is a bit damp. I think somebody must have left it out last night, because we can't touch it off at all. So some of the boys thought if we were for to burn the place a bit first it might go up that way. D'ye know!

DOBELLE: That seems quite a practical notion.

WILLIE: So they sent me up to commandeer a few tins of petrol. There's a couple in the shed by the sea wall, we thought was Mr Tausch's.

DOBELLE: I see.

WILLIE: We'll pay for them, of course. That's what I want to do.

DOBELLE: Just what I would have expected of you, Willie.

WILLIE: Let me see now. 1s 3d a gallon – two gallons a tin – two times 1s 3d is . . .

DOBELLE: 1s 3d from the pump, Willie. 1s 3½d in the tin.

WILLIE: Aw, that's right. One and threepence ha'penny, it is. Two one and threepence ha'pennys is two and seven, and two tins will be twice seven are fourteen, one and two – five and twopence. Isn't that right? [*He counts the money.*]

TAUSCH [*pulling himself together*]: I think I ought to say that one of the tins is not quite full.

DOBELLE: Very handsome of you, Tausch, I'm sure.

WILLIE: Oh, is that so? [*He considers.*] Ah, well, we'll take it all the same. Or supposing we make it the even five bob? [*TAUSCH inclines his head and receives the money.*] And I'm sure you know how sorry we are to have to trouble you, sir. But orders is orders. D'ye know. [*Confidentially.*] And you can have the Fire Brigade out in no time.

TAUSCH: I see. [*He looks round the room and notes the telephone.*] You say you are a soldier. May I speak to your commanding officer?

WILLIE: Oh, I don't think so, sir. This is all very secret, d'ye know.

DOBELLE: Don't be silly, Willie. We all know who it is. Ask Mr Blake to come in and have a drink.

WILLIE: Well, sir . . . I don't know if . . .

DOBELLE: Come in, Darrell, for God's sake.

[DARRELL BLAKE *enters. He is a young man of about twenty-eight with great grace and charm of manner. He is well dressed in an ordinary lounge suit and wears an overcoat, but no hat. He has an air of reckless indifference which – at a distance – is rather fascinating. There is no external evidence of any weapon about his person. The quick nervous movements of his hands betray a highly-strung and sensitive disposition. He carries a small parcel under his arm.*]

BLAKE: Did somebody mention refreshments? Well, that's always a pleasure. [*He bows.*] Ah! [*He blesses the decanter.*] *Benedictus benedicat.*

DOBELLE: Herr Tausch – Mr Blake. Let me pour you out something.

BLAKE: *Sehr angenehm, Herr Tausch.*

TAUSCH [*crossly*]: Good day.

BLAKE: Enough, enough, coz. What will the visitor think of me?

DOBELLE: Sit down, Darrell. [*He goes to the model railway and works with it.*]

BLAKE: Thank you, but I only sit on formal occasions. This is a strictly informal one. Herr Tausch will appreciate.

TAUSCH: I quite appreciate.

BLAKE: I knew you would. Here's health. [*He drinks.*] I'm sorry now we sent Willie in to you. I can see that there's only been a sordid family scene. By the way, I hope you don't think that Willie is our show desperado? Did you, Herr Tausch?

TAUSCH: I hardly know what to think.

BLAKE: Then don't bother at all. Thought is shocking bad for the brain. You should be a man of action like me, Herr Tausch. Terribly desperate, I assure you. You should see the blood I've spilt in my time!

TAUSCH: Mr Blake, I am in no mood for flippancy. I insist upon knowing at once whether it is seriously intended by you or by anybody else to interfere with my Power House?

BLAKE: Why, most seriously. Hannibal is at the gates! You didn't think we were pulling your leg, I hope?

TAUSCH: Then it is true what this man says?

BLAKE: That the wicked shall be burned with fire? Oh yes! Unfortunately it rained last night, and rain is damn bad for explosives, when left in Willie's charge. So you see us temporarily embarrassed.

TAUSCH: Then I go to the Power House, and I will see that nothing of the kind occurs.

BLAKE: Back, back, Don Rodrigo! Regretfully not. For the moment, please regard that as out of the question.

TAUSCH: You propose to hold me by force?

BLAKE: That's right. Quite inexcusable.

TAUSCH: But – but why?

BLAKE [airily]: Oh, Revolution.

TAUSCH: What do you mean?

BLAKE: Just that.

TAUSCH: Revolution! What do you mean? That is just a word!

BLAKE: A beautiful word. So few people appreciate beautiful words nowadays!

WILLIE: Up the Rebels! That's all, d'ye know.

BLAKE: Willie, I think we've had enough of you. Outside

and guard something. We've got a better idea than we had. Where's George, coz?

[WILLIE *goes out.*]

DOBELLE: I'm not sure. Across in the Armoury, I suppose.

BLAKE: This will be a great night for George. The consummation of a lifetime of devotion. Excuse me, while I bring the good news to Aix.

[*He goes.* TAUSCH *is galvanized into activity. He springs to the door and makes sure that nobody is about. Then with a finger to his lips he beckons to* DOBELLE.]

TAUSCH: S-sh! There are men out there. Keep them engaged three minutes, and I will call assistance. See. *Wo ist das Telefonbuch?*

[*He hurries to the telephone and* DOBELLE *indicates the directory on a side table.* TAUSCH *feverishly turns over the pages and then waves* DOBELLE *away. The latter goes to the door, pauses, looks out, then in, shakes his head and finally disappears.* TAUSCH *throws the book away impatiently and takes up the receiver. After a while he glances out of the window and rattles the instrument.*]

TAUSCH: *Allo, Allo! Mein Gott!*

[*He rattles again. The* AUNT *enters carrying her bicycle. He slams down the receiver and turns away in affected innocence.*]

AUNT: Oh no, nobody would pay any attention to me. But maybe they'll listen now. The hour of the poor and the defenceless and the downtrodden comes sooner or later. The dynamos are turning. [*Shouting as she goes upstairs*]: But the proud in their pride shall be laid low. They didn't account for everything. Not for everything!

[*She goes into her room. The* GERMAN *makes sure that she is gone and returns hastily to the telephone. From upstairs the click of the typewriter starts once again. At last he gets a response.*]

TAUSCH [*in a loud whisper*]: *Allo! Allo!* Yes, give me the police – caserne. No, I cannot speak louder . . . What? I do not know the number. Surely you can – No – *Gott in Himmel!* Never mind the Enquiries . . . I want the Military – Troops – *Hilfe* – I say, are you listening? Allo! [*There is a distant burst of laughter from outside. Disconcerted, he glances out of the window before continuing.*] *Allo!* . . . Are you there? . . . *Allo? Allo!*

[WILLIE *enters quietly.* TAUSCH *holds the receiver behind him, breathing heavily, with thoughts of violence in his mind.*]

WILLIE: Did you press button 'A'? [*Pause.*] Maybe I could get it for you. I know the girl below. What is it you want? The Fire Brigade, I suppose? [*He takes the receiver from the speechless* GERMAN.] Well, take my tip and – and – Hello, Miss, is that you? Oh, I'm well, how are ya? . . . Oh, I will indeed. Looka, will you give me double two double two one . . . thanks very much . . . [*To* TAUSCH]: And I tell you what, you'd better give a call to the Guards. There's often a lot of rough sorts and tinkers, you know, that do be hanging around the place where there's a fire. They'd be out in half an hour. Would you like to speak to them yourself? Hello, Miss . . . [*He bangs the receiver.*] Aye, for God's sake, can you not get me the Fire Brigade!

[*The* GERMAN *drops into a chair with a string of expletives. A ship hoots in the river. The turbines hum merrily in the distance through the open door.*]

SWIFT CURTAIN

ACT TWO

This room was once the premises of the Army Ordnance Corps, but it is now used (officially) as a store for the Coast Life Saving Service and (unofficially) as a dumping place for old trunks and furniture belonging to the Dobelle family. There is a wide stone hearth over which the Royal Arms are still to be seen. To the rear is a big double door and a high barred window. Numerous Government circulars relating to distress signals at sea, fog-horns, and the like are pinned and pasted upon the walls, together with a picture of a full-rigged sailing ship cut from a tobacco advertisement. There is a desk against the wall near the window on which are a couple of ledgers. On the one side, opposite the fireplace, is a workman's bench covered with tools, amongst which stand four polished four-inch projectiles. From a door upon this side protrudes something that might be the muzzle of a gun. The room is full of coils of tarred rope, collapsible wooden tripods, a few big life-saving rockets and numerous lanterns of all sizes and shapes. Amongst the stored furniture is a cottage piano, and one or two pictures, all of which are covered with sacking, and on the wall, plainly visible to all, is a large kitchen clock. It stands at five to nine, and keeps going throughout the scene.

[*When the Curtain rises,* CAPTAIN POTTS *is seated on a high stool with his back to the audience, making entries in one of the ledgers, and* GEORGE *is seated near the bench binding the stopper of a glass bottle, into which has been inserted a model of a full-rigged ship.* BLANAID *is seated on the ground beside him. The scene commences about six minutes before the conclusion of Act I.*]

GEORGE: Well, kid, we got into Cape Town, and the Captain he drew a chalk line across the deck abaft the fiddley door and he said to me: 'Quartermaster,' he said, 'the Doctor and

I are going ashore on important business. See that none of those women cross that line.' 'Ay, ay, sir,' said I. So off he and the Doctor went in a hansom cab.

BLANAID: And how many women had you on board?

GEORGE: Hundred and thirty-two. All cooks and house-maids. Government emigrants for Sydney. Never such a cargo known before, my dear.

BLANAID: Well, what happened then?

GEORGE: Well, I sat at the end of the gangway chatting with the little brown-eyed one, and by and by along comes the one called Scotch Annie, at the head of twenty-five whopping great females. 'Annie,' said I, 'you can't go ashore. Captain's orders.' 'George,' said Annie, 'we like you. You're a good sort. And me and these girls don't want to have to sock you one on the jaw.' 'O.K., Annie,' said I, 'I like you too.' And with that up the gangway and ashore they went and the whole hundred and thirty-two after them. All but the little brown-eyed one who stayed chatting with me.

BLANAID: And did they ever come back?

GEORGE: Come back! About an hour later up drives a hansom cab at the gallop with the Captain and the Doctor hanging out and shouting bloody murder. 'Quartermaster,' yells the Captain, 'what the hell does this mean? Whole town's had to close down. Those damn women are every-where.' And then up drives another hansom cab with two policemen and one cook in it. [*He gets up and acts the part with many gestures.*] 'Emigrant from the *Triumph*, sir.' Shove her on board. Salute. Off. Another hansom cab. Two more policemen. Two housemaids. 'Emigrants from the *Triumph*, sir.' Shove 'em on board. Salute. Off. All night. Hansom cabs. Policemen. Cooks and housemaids. Shove 'em on board. Salute. Off. Sailed next morning twenty-nine short. Next year the Boer War.

POTTS: Will you fire a rocket at the Greystones drill?

GEORGE: Greystones? When's that?

POTTS: Wednesday is when you said. Them rockets cost seven pounds apiece.

GEORGE: Um. Lots of kids at Greystones usually. Better let them have a rocket, old man. They like 'em.

BLANAID: May I come and watch you practising, George?

GEORGE: Delighted, kid. Like to go across in the breeches buoy? It's quite safe.

BLANAID: Oh, I'd love to. May I?

GEORGE: Wednesday, then, at Greystones. Artificial respiration too.

[WILLIE *enters and* BLANAID *rises.*]

WILLIE: May I come in?

GEORGE: Of course. Take a seat.

WILLIE: Ah, I won't sit down, thanks very much. I'm on active service, d'ye know.

BLANAID: I knew it was only you, Willie. What's happening?

WILLIE: Nothing much, miss. Mr Blake is over there now – talking.

BLANAID: Oh, Darry? Who to?

WILLIE: Ah, to no one special, miss. They were all talking when I left them.

BLANAID: What were they talking about?

WILLIE: They didn't say, miss.

BLANAID: Then I'm going over to see. Oh, hello!
    [*She meets* BLAKE *in the doorway.*]

BLAKE: And how is my friend Blanaid?

BLANAID: Very well, thank you. You haven't been to see us for years.

BLAKE: I know. But I want to atone for my past with a present. [*He hands her a small parcel.*]

BLANAID: Oh, Darry. [*She examines it.*] I'm so glad there's paper round it. Do you mind if I don't open it for a little?

BLAKE: Of course not. That's much the best part of a present.

BLANAID: I can't imagine what it is. It feels very interesting.

BLAKE: It's really most commonplace. Hello, George. Good evening, Captain.

GEORGE: Well, Blake, old man. Some time since we've seen you.

BLAKE: Yes. I've been rather busy lately. And, by the way, it's you I really want.

GEORGE: Anything to oblige, Darry.

BLAKE: Concerning this loud-speaker of yours we've heard so much about.

AUNT [off]: . . . proud in their pride shall be laid low. They didn't account for everything. Not for everything.

GEORGE: The gun, you mean? Why, man, she's a beauty. Want to see her?

BLAKE: What do you suppose that was?

BLANAID: It sounds like Auntie next door. [BLAKE smiles.] What's the joke, Darry?

BLAKE: She must be abusing poor Tausch. Can you see?
    [BLANAID goes to the door and looks out to the side.]

BLAKE: Have you met Tausch, George?

GEORGE: Oh yes. Potts and I were just giving him a drink about half an hour ago. Peculiar chap, I thought. Still we've got to make allowances for these foreigners. Come on, Potts. Let's get the cover off the gun for Darrell. [They go off.]

BLAKE: Listen, Willie, never mind the petrol. This job is worthy of a bit of style, so we're going to land a shot in the place with the gun. Besides, we want to please the old men.

WILLIE: The gun? Oh, that'll be very interesting for the boys.

BLAKE: Well, what's happening?

BLANAID: He's telephoning.

BLAKE: No! [DOBELLE enters.]

DOBELLE: Really this is too bad. I will not have my guests baited like this. The man's ringing up town.

BLAKE: Marvellous. [*They all crowd round the door and look out.*]

DOBELLE: It mayn't be so marvellous for you when somebody comes out.

BLAKE: By God! He's telephoning all right.

BLANAID: Golly, isn't he excited.

BLAKE: Willie, go across and ask if you can help.

WILLIE: I will indeed, Mr Blake. [*He goes.*]

BLAKE: Watch now everybody. Three to one in pounds that he hits Willie on the jaw. [BLANAID *and* BLAKE *laugh heartily.*]

DOBELLE: It's all very well to laugh. But what's going to happen when Lanigan gets out?

BLAKE: I don't care a damn for Lanigan. What sort of a fool do you suppose that German takes me for? Ringing up town when he thinks he's got me out of the way. And now I suppose he'll come across and try to distract us for half an hour with bright, helpful conversation until the lorries can get out with the Staters. I do dislike having my intelligence insulted.

DOBELLE: Darrell, this is intolerable behaviour. You know quite well what it will mean in the end.

BLAKE: Listen, I've got an idea. Is the tide out, my dear?

BLANAID: Yes. Why?

BLAKE: Then I think I'll give Mr Tausch all the cat and mouse he wants and a bit to spare. We'll get the gun out on the sea wall, loaded and trained on the works, and then, by God, Tausch shall have all the distracting conversation he asks for. We'll keep him on the hop for ten, fifteen, twenty minutes until we hear the rumble of the lorries. God, what a scheme! I'll be laughing for months. The rumble of the lorries, and the Bosch thinking he's caught us. And then bang goes the gun, up go the Works to hell, and off we trot across the sand to the shore on the far side. What do you think of that?

DOBELLE: Exactly. And leave us to take the consequences.

BLAKE: They can't take the lorries off the road. We'll have them on toast.

DOBELLE: You know perfectly well what it will mean. The ruin of our privacy for weeks. The enquiries – the cross-examination – the statements – the alibis! Some of these days, my boy, I damn well will make a statement and where will you be then?

BLAKE: Don't worry. You'll have much the best part of the evening's entertainment. You'll be able to see the German's face. I'd give my soul for that. I do hope Willie hasn't discouraged him.

BLANAID [*opening her parcel and disclosing a small book*]: Oh, how lovely! Did you have to buy it, Darry?

BLAKE: There. That's all the thanks a criminal ever gets! I always said you were badly brought up.

BLANAID: The Girl Guide's Diary. [*Laughing.*] Oh, it's perfect.

DOBELLE [*grumbling round amongst the Dobelle impedimenta*]: Insufferable! Monstrous! Nobody has ever any consideration for me.

[*A ship hoots in the river.*]

BLANAID: With a pencil and everything. It's full of useful information.

BLAKE: Come on, George. About this gun. May I show it to the boys?

GEORGE [*reappearing*]: Only too delighted, old man. Know anything about guns?

BLAKE: No, but I'm always ready to learn. This is the dangerous end, I suppose?

GEORGE: In theory, old man. At present we can't say more. Come along, Potts. We'll have to show him.

[POTTS *appears.*]

BLANAID: I suppose I could be a Lone Guide if I learnt all these knots?

DOBELLE: Of course, you must upset the fellow when he's my guest. Some of these things seem familiar.

GEORGE: This gun is what we call a muzzle loading, four-inch-slow-firing-Potts-shot. Now explain, Potts. You've got it all learnt off.

POTTS [*in a steady sing-song*]: Well, sir, beginning at this end, first the steel barrel is strengthened with wrought iron 'oops shrunk over one another so that the inner toob or barrel is placed in a state of compression and the outer portions is in a state of tension.

BLAKE: You don't say.

POTTS: Furthermore, by forming the outer parts of wrought iron bar coiled round a mandrel and then welding the coil into a solid 'oop, the fibre of the iron is arranged what we calls circumferentially, and is thus in the best position to resist the stress.

DOBELLE: Who the devil brings all these things of mine over here? No wonder I never can find anything!

BLAKE: One moment – just before you go any further. You mentioned a mandrel. Now, what exactly is that?

POTTS: A mandrel?

[*An uncomfortable pause.*]

GEORGE: Better come right inside, old man. Able to explain better there. Eh, Potts?

POTTS: Inside? Oh, yaw. Much better inside.

[*They go out.* DOBELLE *has taken the sacking partially off one of the pictures, disclosing the portrait of a young woman dressed in the clothes of about thirty years ago.* POTTS *returns to collect a corkscrew and a couple of glasses from the bench.*]

POTTS: Forgotten something, George. [*He goes.*]

[*There are sounds of movement off followed by the clink of glasses.* BLANAID *stands looking at her father.* WILLIE *enters.*]

WILLIE: Where's Mr Blake?

BLAKE [*off*]: Busy, Willie. [*Pop of a cork.*]

WILLIE: Oh, are you there? He doesn't seem to want anything. He sent me across and says he'll be after me.

[*He goes into the adjoining room. There is the sound of flowing liquid.*]

DOBELLE: Now there's something I've been looking for for months. How did it get here?

BLANAID: I don't know, father. A lot of the things from the house get left over here.

DOBELLE: Well nobody has any business to take it, no matter how full the place is.

[DOBELLE *stares out of the window. Siphon off.* BLANAID *approaches him tentatively.*]

BLANAID: Father. . . . Did you see what Darry gave me?

DOBELLE: No.

BLANAID: It's a diary . . . I love it.

DOBELLE: You'll lose it, I expect.

BLANAID: No, I won't. Guides don't lose things. . . . Father, do you think that giving presents to a person is a sign of friendship?

DOBELLE: I really don't know.

BLANAID: I think so. I haven't very many friends, I'm afraid. . . . [*Silence.*] . . . Daddy, would this diary be of any use to you?

[DOBELLE *turns his head and looks at her for a moment.*]

BLANAID: You don't want it?

DOBELLE [*shakes his head and turns away*]: No, thank you.

BLANAID: I see. [*Choking it back.*] Well . . . I think . . . I want something . . . in my room.

[*She turns and runs out.*]

POTTS [*off*]: The castings are annealed by placing them in a furnace or hoven until red 'ot, then allowing them to cool gradyerly. The exterior of the body must be ground by a hemery wheel or turned on a lathe. [*Pop of cork.*] 'Ere's looking at yer. [*Pause. Then briskly*]: The groove for the driving band is also turned an' the fuse 'ole fitted with a gun-metal bush.

BLAKE [*off*]: And the same to you.

THE MOON IN THE YELLOW RIVER

[TAUSCH *enters. He has an air of suppressed excitement and crosses swiftly to* DOBELLE.]

TAUSCH: *Ach*, so you are here! [*He whispers loudly*]: Listen, *fünf-und-zwanzig Minuten*. When I have got rid of the young man I call the Barracks. They come in lorries. Twenty-five minutes and all will be well.

DOBELLE: I expected as much. This is all most distasteful. [*He goes to the door.*]

TAUSCH [*misunderstanding him*]: *Nein, nein.* Courage, *mein Freund.* Courage! See, until nine hours thirty! *Frisch gewagt ist halb gewonnen*, eh, *Kamerad!*

    [*Enter* BLAKE, GEORGE, POTTS, *and* WILLIE. *They go to the shell cases.*]

BLAKE: How many did you say you've got?

TAUSCH [*conversationally*]: *Ach*, so here we are!

GEORGE: Hello, Splosch, old man. Four.

POTTS: The last one needs a bit o' greasing. We only got it done last week.

BLAKE: Four. A beautiful number. Like the gospels.

DOBELLE [*calling*]: Columba, come over here, please.

GEORGE: We'll have more in a year or so. Takes time to get down to them, you know.

BLAKE: Four are quite enough to save our souls. Do you mind if we take everything outside?

GEORGE: Not at all, old man. What's it all about?

BLAKE: Crime, George! Enough said, for your own sake. To-night I am Dick Deadeye, the boy burglar! I'll call the boys to help to get it out the door. Willie, you bring one of those things.

DOBELLE: Columba, will you kindly come when I call you. [*He disappears out the door, carrying the picture with him.*]

TAUSCH: Er, perhaps I also can assist in some way.

BLAKE: Of course, Herr Tausch. We were just saying you would. Bright, helpful conversation.

WILLIE: Will I take this one?

BLAKE: Any one. And for God's sake be careful. Remember they go off.

WILLIE: Oh, I'll walk like a cat.

[*Half-way to the door, the shell spins in his grasp, he catches it again, loses it once more, and finally lets it fall.* TAUSCH *drops flat on his face.* BLAKE *covers his head with an arm.* GEORGE *and* POTTS *fall into a locked embrace. The shell bounces dully and then lies still. Pause.*]

WILLIE: Oh! I dropped it.

BLAKE: He dropped it! He tells us he dropped it.

[GEORGE *and* POTTS *come slowly forward and bend over the object on the ground.*]

GEORGE: That was strange, Potts.

POTTS: Don't understand that, George. [*They prod it gingerly. Nothing happens.*]

WILLIE: Did it not go off?

BLAKE: O God, give me patience!

GEORGE: Should do better than that, old man. [*He picks it up and shakes it to an ear.*] I don't know. Some carelessness somewhere.

POTTS: Watcher mean, carelessness?

GEORGE: Did you bring the water to the boil?

POTTS: Of course I brought the water to the boil.

GEORGE: Doesn't look like it, old man.

WILLIE: I hope I didn't break it on you.

POTTS [*indignantly gets out a dog-eared notebook*]: There's the nitrate, ain't it – mercurous nitrate, sol-soluble in 'undred an' thirty times its weight o' boiling water.

GEORGE: Well let's bring it over and have a look.

POTTS: 'Ave as many looks as you like, but I don't like them insinuations, George. D'ye think I don't know 'ow ter boil water?

GEORGE: Now, now, Potts, there's no use crying over spilt milk. Maybe the stuff's not shaken down in the bag.

POTTS: Well, it's not my job to shake it, is it?

BLAKE [*dusting himself*]: So much for Matthew. I suppose we may expect equally good performances from the other three?

GEORGE: No, no, not at all. You see, this one was the first we made. Probably a bit on the old side by now. Or maybe Potts here. . . .

POTTS [*threateningly*]: Atcher!

BLAKE: In any event, we'll excuse you, Willie. Go and help the boys to get that thing out. I'll handle the next myself.

WILLIE [*most willingly*]: Right ye are, Mr Blake. Where's it to go?

BLAKE [*in a low voice*]: Across the yard behind that parapet. And then you're to train the muzzle very carefully through one of those loopholes on to the roof of the turbine-house. Now, do you understand me? Because say so, for God's sake, if you don't.

WILLIE: Oh, I do indeed. That'll be very interesting. [*To the earnest workers at the bench, as he passes*]: I hope it'll be all right. [*He goes.*]

TAUSCH: *Alles zu seiner Zeit*, Mr Blake. You think it is necessary for us to risk our poor lives again?

BLAKE: It's all for the cause, you know. Did you see my glass anywhere?

[TAUSCH *fetches it and fills another for himself, which, however, he does not drink.*]

TAUSCH: I would like so much to talk with you for a little. To ask you some questions about yourself.

BLAKE [*smiling*]: Well, why not. There's no hurry is there?

TAUSCH: Oh no. No hurry at all.

GEORGE: Try the screw in the base-plug.

POTTS: D'ye know that's the centrifugal bolt.

BLAKE: I suppose they're all right with that damn thing?

TAUSCH: We are in the hands of One above.

VOICES [*off*]:
  Come on in, boys.
  That's right, get the door open.

Ay, will you look where you're going?

BLAKE: Well, what do you want to know about me?

TAUSCH: Mr Blake, I am very glad I have met you. I think you are the most interesting person I have known since I have come to your most interesting country.

BLAKE: Oh, come now. Flattery.

TAUSCH: Yes, indeed. But, believe me, it is not quite the compliment. For, you see, I am much more interested in my enemies than in my friends. And I feel that you are my enemy.

BLAKE: I only hope, Herr Tausch, a foeman worthy of your steel.

TAUSCH: I think so. I think so.

BLAKE [*raising his glass*]: Then may the worst man win. [TAUSCH *bows and drinks a sip also.*]

GEORGE: Take the needle pellet out of another one. This is no good.

POTTS: Picric, ain't it?

TAUSCH: They tell me you are a political idealist, Mr Blake. Now tell me, please, what is it you object to in the present state of the country?

BLAKE: Oh, innumerable things.

TAUSCH: You insist upon the outward symbols of independence and are not content with just the substance. Am I right?

BLAKE: You've been reading our pamphlets, Herr Tausch.

TAUSCH: You see, I have every sympathy with your National Movement.

BLAKE [*snapping his fingers*]: Personally I don't give that for the National Movement. I'm not one of those who are eager to spill their blood for the colouring on maps. We're taught better things than that nowadays. *Ad Majorem Dei Gloriam!*

TAUSCH: So? The slogan of the Jesuits. I too am a Catholic. We should be able to understand each other.

BLAKE: Now don't make me laugh.

[*For some time* WILLIE *has been pushing vigorously at the muzzle of the gun.*]

A VOICE [*off*]: Say when you're ready to shove.

WILLIE: Ah God! haven't I been shoving for the last ten minutes.

[*The gun is heaved out of sight.* WILLIE *falls after it.*]

TAUSCH: But, Mr Blake, if you are not working for the National Movement, may I ask why you are here?

BLAKE: National movements are only a means to an end. We're not such parochial politicians as you seem to take us for.

TAUSCH: But why, then? Why all this?

BLAKE: Why not? Look here, Herr Tausch, you are our guest, and I declare that in a way I like you. Let me give you a word of advice. Don't let yourself be deceived by life. She's fooling you.

TAUSCH: In what way, pray?

BLAKE: My God, man, go out and take a look at your works and then ask yourself that question again. Listen to the noise of your turbines and then come back and give me any adequate reason for it all. The rest of the world may be crazy, but there's one corner of it yet, thank God, where you and your ludicrous machinery haven't turned us all into a race of pimps and beggars.

TAUSCH: Machinery, my dear sir, does not make pimps and beggars.

BLAKE: It makes Proletarians. Is that any better?

[*A stream of pieces of metal falls off the bench.* GEORGE *and* POTTS, *with many mutterings, get down on their knees to pick them up.*]

TAUSCH: But, Mr Blake, must we not have some regard for progress?

BLAKE: My good man, how do you know what progress is? Tell me, if you dare.

TAUSCH: Well, perhaps I may put it this way without offence. Surely you must admit that there are such things as backward countries?

BLAKE: There are countries where, incredible as it may seem to you, some of us prefer to live.

WILLIE [*off*]: If you go through there you'll be stuck in the jamb of the door.

TAUSCH: You don't think me rude, I hope. I am afraid you may think me a little patronizing in coming to work for you here, and you resent it. But –

BLAKE: My dear fellow, set your mind at rest on that point. I resent nothing. I am sorry for you, that's all, as I am sorry for everybody I see being imposed upon.

TAUSCH: Mr Dobelle has also expressed his sorrow for me this evening. I assure you it is a misplaced condolence.

BLAKE: If man has anything to boast of that the ant, the bee and the mole haven't got, surely it's his greater capacity for enjoying life. To me it is progress just to live – to live more consciously and more receptively. Herr Tausch, do you never see yourself as rather a ridiculous figure trying to catch life in a blast-furnace?

TAUSCH: It seems to me that the blast-furnace is just the thing that leaves us all the freer to enjoy life.

BLAKE: Excuse me – does it leave *you* any the freer? Does it leave your dirty workmen any the freer? That's just where you allow yourself to be deceived. It's just another shackle on your limbs, and a self-inflicted one at that. I might be like you, Herr Tausch, if I chose, and this country might be like yours if you had your way. But I don't choose, and you won't have your way. Because we intend to keep one small corner of the globe safe for the unfortunate human race.

TAUSCH: Very interesting. And so you are a machine wrecker? We are engaged in a Kulturkampf. Well, I have heard of such before. You are a man of courage, Mr Blake.

BLAKE: To challenge you? Tausch said 'Let there be light,' And the evening and the morning were the first day.

TAUSCH: There have been others.

BLAKE: Elsewhere maybe. But here we believe that the dawn will break in the west. You bring us light from the wrong direction.

[GEORGE *is holding the shell, and* POTTS *is rapping it smartly on the nose with a wooden mallet.*]

GEORGE: Give it a good hard one, Potts old man.

BLAKE: Really, I do think this has gone far enough. Can't you do that somewhere else?

GEORGE: Quite safe, old chap.

BLAKE: Look out! You'll spoil that suit of yours, Potts. If you want a double anniversary, do try a bit nearer to the Works.

POTTS: My suit? You know, George, I'd forgotten all about the poor old missus.

GEORGE: There now, you've reminded the old fellow!

BLAKE: Anything to take his mind off that damn bomb. And look here, what have you been doing to this other one? It's all in bits.

GEORGE: Had to take out the needle pellet. And she just came apart in my hands.

BLAKE: Damn it, then there's only two left!

POTTS: Think I'll have to go and have a drink, George.

GEORGE: I can well believe it, Captain. Come along with me. [*To* BLAKE.] Shouldn't have mentioned that about his suit, you know. I told you not to. [*He leaves by a door on the fireplace side.*]

BLAKE: Oh, do cheer up, Potts. Did you ever tell Herr Tausch the story?

POTTS [*hesitating in the door*]: I don't think as 'ow I did.

TAUSCH: I am sure it would be very painful for the Herr Kapitän on such a day as this.

BLAKE: Not at all. We often discuss it. You should listen to this, Tausch. It's rather illuminating. Go on, Potts. Here's a fresh cosmopolitan mind for you.

POTTS: Well, you see, sir, we was all out in the old *Mermaid*, and we found out we only 'ad the one lifebelt as soon as she turned out to be sprung. Well, I was for drawing lots for it. But George, 'e says, 'No, Potts, women and children first, Potts,' 'e says. So I says, 'You're right, George.' So we fixes the lifebelt around the old missus and pitches her overboard.

TAUSCH: Ah, your ship was sinking!

POTTS: Well, yes, sir, in a way. So we thought at the time. But that's just the queer thing, sir, for when the fog lifted and we could see what was what, there we was agr'ound in about 'alf a fathom 'ard by Fairview.

TAUSCH: *Ach*, so. That was fortunate for you. You escaped?

POTTS: Sure. We just waded ashore. All but the old missus, poor soul. We didn't get 'er till the next day.

TAUSCH: She was safe in the lifebelt?

POTTS: Sure she was safe in it. Floating a cable or two off Salthill. The wrong ways up. Poor Maggie. I often wonders whether we was wrong, sir. George 'e says not, and 'e ought ter know. But sometimes on 'er anniversary I thinks of poor Maggie, and, you know, I 'as my doubts. I do indeed. [*He shakes his head and follows* GEORGE *off*.]

BLAKE: Well? You don't feel inclined to laugh?

TAUSCH: Mr Blake, I never feel inclined to laugh at a man because his wife is dead. I am amazed that a man of some sensibility such as yourself could be so cruel.

BLAKE [*thinks for a moment and at last raises his glass*]: To Death, Herr Tausch, that makes the whole world kin. [*He drinks.*] There's nothing cruel about her. [*He sits.*] Quite the reverse. [*There is another pause while he sinks into a brown study.*]

TAUSCH: Come, my friend. Perhaps I have been unjust. I am sorry.

BLAKE: It's all right. I'm partially intoxicated, that's all. [*Angry voices rise outside.*]

VOICES:

A bucketful will do.

Try it the other way round.

Ah, will you leave it alone?

Etc.

BLAKE [*pulling himself together*]: What are those damn fellows up to now?

TAUSCH: Wait, I will see. [*They both look at the clock.*]

BLAKE [*rising*]: We can't fool about here any longer. *Fronta capillata*, as the elder Cato says. If Matthew and Mark fail us, then Luke must do the trick.

[BLAKE *takes the third shell and goes out.* TAUSCH *hastily fills his glass from the bottle and hurries after him.*]

TAUSCH [*following*]: Mr Blake, you have forgotten your glass.

WILLIE [*off*]: Ay, will ye looka. I say the bloody thing goes the other way round. [*Altercations till* BLAKE'S *voice quietens them. After a moment* DOBELLE *and* AUNT COLUMBA *come in.*]

DOBELLE: I don't care how full the house is. Nobody has any business to leave any of my things over here.

AUNT: Don't raise your voice at me, please. You can't intimidate me with loud speeches.

DOBELLE: I wish to God I could intimidate somebody in this house.

AUNT: Well, now that we're on the subject of intimidation, what have you been saying to Blanaid?

DOBELLE: Nothing. Why?

AUNT: She's retired to her room in tears. Whatever it is this time, I've had to tell you before that you're doing that child a great injustice.

DOBELLE: Well, hasn't she done me an injustice?

AUNT: You mean – Mary? How can you blame her for that? She didn't ask to be born.

DOBELLE: It seems to me that she was most insistent about being born.

AUNT: Roddy, you're unbalanced on that subject.

DOBELLE: Next you're going to tell me that I'm off my head, I suppose.

AUNT: Sometimes I wonder. But that doesn't make any difference to your duty to instruct her.

DOBELLE: Don't I leave that to you?

AUNT: Yes. But you don't allow me to teach her about you-know-where.

[*She points downwards.*]

DOBELLE: I don't see why that should be an essential part of her instruction.

AUNT: Don't be ridiculous, Roddy. Doesn't the Bible say: 'Suffer the little children to come unto me'? Well, if one adopts your absurd attitude, supposing they won't come, where can you tell them to go to?

DOBELLE: My dear Columba, if your instruction depends on that – as indeed all instruction ultimately does – then it only confirms what I say – that ignorance is bliss.

AUNT: She's entitled to be told.

DOBELLE: Well, I won't have it. And if I find she knows, you can leave this house.

AUNT: It is every parent's duty and privilege to tell his child about that.

DOBELLE: I deny all duties and privileges where Blanaid is concerned. I will feed and clothe her, but there my interests end.

AUNT: What possible complaint can you have against her? She's a most mild-mannered child.

DOBELLE: Her existence . . . that was bought and paid for at Pressburg. Isn't that enough?

AUNT: That's a most outrageous thing to say. I'd like to know what Mary would think.

DOBELLE: Columba, you're a most unscrupulous woman. What right have you to bring Mary into it when you know I can't bear the subject?

AUNT: Well I can't say I've ever noticed any great tact on your part where my feelings are concerned. Aren't you always hinting to me about mowing-machines?

DOBELLE: Be quiet. They're coming back.

AUNT: I won't be quiet.

DOBELLE: S-sh!

[*They continue to converse in low undertones amongst the luggage.* TAUSCH *enters. He smiles nervously as they glare at him, and he crosses swiftly to the door through which* GEORGE *and* POTTS *have gone out. He looks out and then closes it, coming back centre as* BLAKE *enters rather loquaciously tipsy.*]

BLAKE: Come and show us which way up this – oh! Where's George?

TAUSCH: He is not here.

[BLAKE *looks out the wrong door.*]

BLAKE: Oh, hell!

TAUSCH: Well, Mr Blake. You were to tell me what you thought of me.

BLAKE: Was I? Well, I'll tell you how I regard you. As a demon pantechnicon driver. Old worlds into new quarters, by road, rail, and sea.

TAUSCH [*with a look at the clock*]: But surely that is a most praiseworthy occupation?

BLAKE: Maybe. Do what you like with your own world. But I insist that you leave me mine. I am Persephone, weary of memory, putting poppies in my hair.

TAUSCH: This world is neither yours nor mine. It belongs to all these people. Have you the right to say that I may not help them?

BLAKE: Who else will say it if I don't?

TAUSCH [*laughing*]: Well, I think that they might perhaps have something to say for themselves.

BLAKE: Pooh! [*Then, in poker parlance*]: Well, I'll see you. Let's ask them.

TAUSCH: I agree.

C

BLAKE: The verdict of democracy.

TAUSCH: Free from force or unfair influence.

BLAKE: God bless the dear old people. The majority is always right.

TAUSCH: Mr and Miss Dobelle!

DOBELLE: Still fishing the troubled waters of a dry well, eh?

BLAKE [*shouting at the door*]: Willie! Blanaid!

TAUSCH: It is a matter of great interest. Will you join us? [*Whispers.*] Twelve minutes more.

DOBELLE: Well, I'll listen at any rate.

[*Enter* GEORGE *and* POTTS.]

BLAKE: Oh, here you are. I've been looking for you everywhere. Look here . . .

GEORGE: Hullo, Splosch, old man, still here?

BLAKE: You'd better take the chair, Potts. You're the most impartial.

POTTS: What's all this? [*He sits and smokes his pipe, phlegmatically.* WILLIE *enters.*]

AUNT: I suppose we must have that door open all night regardless of the temperature.

[BLAKE *and* WILLIE *close it.*]

BLAKE: Have you been able to fix that, Willie?

WILLIE: Oh, I think so. It looks all right to me now.

BLAKE [*opening the window and again speaking in a low voice*]: Well, stand there by the window and listen for you-know-what. And the minute you hear them coming tell me at once.

WILLIE: But are we not going to . . .

BLAKE: Do what I tell you, and stop making remarks, Willie. I know what I'm doing.

[WILLIE *stands at the window. For some time* TAUSCH *has been speaking earnestly to* GEORGE.]

GEORGE: But did I ever call you 'Splosch', old man?

TAUSCH: It is a small matter. Just if you can remember.

GEORGE [*ruminatively*]: Tosh – Tush – [*He puts the bottle beside* BLAKE's *chair.*] Good for the voice, old man.

BLAKE: Thank you, George. You'd better keep some minutes, Aunt Columba. This will be nuts and wine to you.

AUNT: Many a minute I've kept that people have regretted when sober.

[*She draws forward a small table and sits down.* BLANAID *comes quietly in and sits on the ground. She takes out her diary and starts to write in it.* BLAKE *rises to his feet.*]

BLAKE: Dearly beloved, the situation is a straightforward one. Our German brother stands indicted before the Bar of this Court on the gravest of charges. He has outraged the sacred person of our beloved Mother – Kathleen-ni-Houlihan. I say let him be condemned and his Works be a deodand. In other words, I propose to blow them up. We leave it to you.

TAUSCH: To express your views without force or unfair influence.

BLAKE: *Nihil obstat.* What are you working at, my dear?

BLANAID: I'm filling in my personal memoranda. [*She produces a tape and takes a few measurements of her span, breadth of thumb, etc.*]

TAUSCH: Perhaps you will let me begin with a few words.

AUNT: Just one moment, please. I understood that this was to be some sort of public discussion. Now it appears to be more like a court martial.

BLAKE: Oh, need we go into that?

AUNT: It is of importance as to who should speak first.

TAUSCH: It is all the same. It makes no difference.

AUNT: Excuse me, it makes a very big difference.

TAUSCH: It is just what you choose to call it. That is of no importance.

AUNT: Herr Tausch, if you call its tail a leg, how many legs do you say a cow has got?

TAUSCH: Really, Miss Dobelle!

AUNT: Answer me, please.

TAUSCH: If you call its tail a leg? Well, five, I suppose.

AUNT: Wrong, four. Because calling its tail a leg doesn't make it one. Blanaid, you're the junior. Begin.

BLANAID: Me? Well, I think it would be a shame to blow them up.

AUNT: Reasons, please, if any.

BLANAID: Because I like Herr Tausch and I think you're all being beastly to him.

BLAKE: For acquittal. Well, that's one point of view. [*Drinks deeply.*]

TAUSCH: Thank you, *mein Herzchen*. It is not a reason that I had expected, but I appreciate it.

AUNT: Now, Willie?

WILLIE: Ah, sure there's no good asking me. I'm on active service.

AUNT: But if you weren't on active service?

WILLIE: I'm always on active service. I took an oath, you know, and I can't go back on that.

TAUSCH: What kind of an oath?

WILLIE: To obey my superior officers, and not to recognize the Government until the Country's free. Isn't this a Government works?

TAUSCH: Pardon me, but what is the difference between the 'Government' and the 'Country'?

[*All laugh.*]

DOBELLE: All the difference in the world if you're out of office. I thought I'd made that clear.

TAUSCH: But, pardon me, Willie. If it were not for your oath, do you not think that to blow up the Works would do a lot of harm to the country?

WILLIE: Ah, it would and it wouldn't. Wouldn't it help a lot of lads out of work if they had for to build them up again? I'm dead against unemployment, d'ye know.

BLAKE: That's enough. Conviction. Who's next?

TAUSCH: But may not the accused speak a word upon his own behalf?

AUNT: Don't interrupt, please. I'm next. And I wish it to be quite clear that I have as yet no personal objection to Herr Tausch.

TAUSCH: I am so glad.

AUNT: He may be a most estimable man for all I know, although he does try to get young girls to go with him to the pictures, and as for his morals, well, they don't concern me. I can be as broadminded as anybody.

TAUSCH: I beg your pardon. . . .

AUNT: Nor have I any objection to any ordinary factory as such. But this building is a Power House, which is quite a different thing. Some people, I know, are inclined to scoff at the significance of Power Houses, and to dismiss them lightly as just a small matter. But it is those very people who before they realize it have become dependent on the very thing they tried to laugh off. They think that they can give them up at any time. But they never can. Never.

TAUSCH: The lady is surely speaking of alcohol!

BLAKE: But this is eloquence, Aunt Columba. There's not a dry eye.

AUNT: Now once you become dependent upon anything, you are the slave of the man who controls it. Expected to bow the knee to some place-hunting industrialist with a small technical education and with neither culture nor religion to guide him. And if anybody thinks I am going to do that he is very greatly mistaken. I will not be dominated or controlled by anybody, and I am very grateful to Darry Blake for what he suggests, although I don't pretend to approve of him in other ways.

BLAKE: Thank you, Aunt Columba. You see, Tausch, I am appreciated too.

TAUSCH: Really, Miss Dobelle, I am none of these things you call me. I do not expect you to bow the knee.

AUNT: Order, please.

TAUSCH: You misunderstand me, I assure you.

AUNT: You are persistently interrupting, Herr Tausch. Please understand I will not be trampled on by you.

BLAKE: Yes, stop trampling on Aunt Columba, Tausch, and sit down. Now, George?

[TAUSCH *shrugs his shoulders and sits down with a glance at the clock.*]

GEORGE: Well, you know I haven't the gift of the gab the way you people have, but when I was in Birmingham I sometimes used to watch all those women and young girls coming in and out of the factories. And, you know, I was touched – more touched than I can say. All those women and young girls having to work night and day, with their poor, pale, pasty faces that they have to make up with rouge and all that, brought tears to my eyes, old man. They ought to be kept out of doors and have proper homes of their own, you know. No life for young girls.

TAUSCH: Then you need not have young girls in your factories.

GEORGE: Got to think of the women, you know, old man. Can't bear to see them suffer.

BLAKE: Two up and one to play. [*He stands.*] Well, George, your young girls will have to thank you for their green fields from this out.

GEORGE: Me? How do you make that out?

BLAKE: You and your gun. That's the idea. Why bother with damp cheddar when the third Evangelist is waiting by the sea wall to do the trick for us.

GEORGE: I say, old man, you don't mean you're thinking of actually firing that gun?

BLAKE: Precisely.

GEORGE: Oh, I didn't know that. Did you, Potts?

POTTS: No. I didn't know that.

BLAKE: My dear man, we've been talking of nothing else all evening.

GEORGE: Oh well, I didn't hear you say that.

BLAKE: You don't seem pleased?

GEORGE: Well, it's all very well, you know. But it's a bit of a surprise. After all, those shells. Took a year each to make. And now to see them go up in a flash! And the gun. Four years' work, old man. Supposing something happens to it?

BLAKE: George, you're not trying to back out, are you?

GEORGE: Well, what do you think, Potts?

POTTS: Oh, I didn't know they was going to take our gun.

GEORGE: We won't get it back, you know. Once they hear about it, it's gone for good.

POTTS: Yes, that's a bit thick, I think.

GEORGE: Anything in reason, old man. But, all these years' work!

BLAKE: George, I'm sorry. We thought you'd be pleased if we used it. But it's too late to change now. That's understood.

GEORGE: Oh, well, I'm against it, then.

POTTS: So'm I.

AUNT: You're in the chair. You've only got a casting vote.

POTTS: Is that so?

AUNT: Definitely.

BLAKE: Then it all depends on you, coz. What's the verdict?

TAUSCH: Yes, Mr Dobelle, it depends on you.

DOBELLE: I'm against you.

TAUSCH: *Davor behüte uns Gott!*

BLAKE: Thumbs down!

DOBELLE: My reasons are –

[*Enter* AGNES *with a tray.*]

AGNES: Of course, if you must sit up all night across here in the cold while the fire is roaring in the sitting-room it's no concern of mine. Here's your tea anyway, and you needn't expect me again this evening, for I'm not coming back till poor Mrs Mulpeter is over her trouble.

BLANAID [*taking the tray*]: Thank you, Agnes.

AGNES: I've a bottleful of Lourdes water and a string of charmed knots to undo. I've unlocked every door in the house and taken the braids out of my hair. If the tide's coming in, it will be a boy, but once it's over the turn – Who left that brown paper and string there? Was it you, Miss Blanaid?

BLANAID: I'm awfully sorry, Agnes. But I'd like the string to practise a few knots with.

DOBELLE: I would like to give you my reasons. . . .

AGNES: You know quite well I must have any brown paper and string. You've no consideration at all. Willie, put that in the drawer of my dresser.

WILLIE: I'm wanted here, Ma.

AGNES: Be off, ye yuck, before I level you.

WILLIE: But Ma, looka . . .

AGNES: Be off, I tell you! [*He runs.*] Good-bye now. The Doctor's on his way up, so I must run.

BLAKE: Agnes, just before you go, may I ask you one question?

AGNES: Well, what is it? You'll have to be quick.

BLAKE: We're thinking of blowing up the Power House. What would you say to that?

AGNES: Now there's another thing. The whirring thrum of them mechanicalisms is very disturbing to poor Mrs Mulpeter. You'll have to stop it and the sooner the better. All I say is, whatever you do, do it quietly or you'll hear from me. Good night so. I'll not be back now till it's over for good and all. [*She goes.*]

DOBELLE [*taking his cup*]: Some day, God willing, I shall strike that woman.

AUNT: There was nothing to prevent you this evening, was there?

DOBELLE: Nothing to prevent me! Sometimes you ask damn silly questions, Columba.

AUNT: There's no need to be any more offensive than usual. If you can't get on with her, why don't you get rid of her?

DOBELLE: You can't get rid of Agnes. She'd only come back under a different name. Once you surrender to servants you have no right to live.

AUNT: She's a very efficient woman.

DOBELLE: She's a damned dragon.

BLAKE: A dragon? Well, St George, they say, was a dishonest beef contractor. I'll find you one of his descendants, coz.

DOBELLE: I have not given you my reasons yet. This man Tausch comes here with the most high-hatted motives and . . .

AUNT [*giving tea to* TAUSCH *and* BLANAID, GEORGE *and* BLAKE *having refused*]: That's all right.

GEORGE: I propose a vote of thanks to the chairman for the very able way he has conducted this meeting.

BLANAID: Hear, hear. [*Clapping.*]

DOBELLE: He appears to be determined to do good in the abstract sense. Now that is an attitude of mind which . . .

POTTS [*pouring his tea into his saucer*]: 'At's aw ri'. But about this 'ere gun . . .

BLAKE [*in front of the arms over the fireplace*]: And talking of Georges brings us to Dei Gratia Rex Imperator Number Five.

DOBELLE: I was once like Herr Tausch here. I too built barrages and constructed power houses, until one day I found myself to be a false friend. So we parted company.

BLAKE: The lion, you know, is really a very middle-class beast. I think that we may disregard the lion. But the unicorn is a most interesting animal.

DOBELLE: I beg your pardon, will you kindly listen to me?

TAUSCH: I am listening, Mr Dobelle.

DOBELLE: But nobody else is. However, I will tell you, Herr Tausch, why we can never be friends. You wish to serve something you call progress. But progress is never achieved by people like you who pursue it. Progress is the fruit of evil men, with sinister motives. You and your kind can only make misery.

TAUSCH: I do not understand.

DOBELLE: I don't blame you. Very few people will see what I mean.

BLAKE: The unicorn is said to be a beast of great virility and of great ferocity. Yet they tell us that he is subdued to gentleness at the sight of a virgin.

DOBELLE: Have you ever studied Aquinas?

[TAUSCH *rises and listens, a smile spreading over his face.*]

BLAKE: A lonely, chaste and noble beast in many ways rather akin to myself.

DOBELLE: Quite so. Aquinas tells us that in order that the blisses of Paradise may be more delightful to them the Blessed in Heaven will be expected to view the tortures of the damned and to rejoice.

[*From outside comes the sound of engines and of distant shouting. Then there is a stampede of men past the window and* BLAKE *springs into activity.*]

BLAKE: Christ, I forgot! Where's Willie? Why didn't he tell me?

[*He rushes to the window and shouts.*]

BLAKE: Hi, wait! Fire the gun first, you fools! Fire the bloody gun, it's all set! Willie . . . you there, d'you hear me? Get back, you goddam imbecile. No, in the fuse hole, curse you. The other end. Quick . . . you've time enough. All right. Got it? Give her hell . . . One . . . two . . .

[*He gets down and covers his ears. Several others do likewise. Eventually there is a dull clank as of falling metal. All straighten up and listen, but there is no further sound.*]

BLAKE: I give it up! Oh, I give it up! Really, this is too much.

VOICES [*off*]: Hi, you! Put up your hands. Stand back there!

GEORGE: Did anything happen?

BLAKE: Did anything happen! Oh, my God!

GEORGE: What's up? He can't have put it in right. Ought to do better than that, you know. Come on, Potts, and we'll see.

[*He opens the door. On the threshold stands a soldier in a green uniform.* GEORGE *and* POTTS *turn on their heels and walk rapidly off into the adjoining room.*]

GEORGE: Oh, excuse me.

[*The* SOLDIER *comes in. He is a man of about thirty-seven, with a pale saturnine face and sunken cheeks. His pale blue eyes contrast strangely with the incipient beard and shock of wiry black hair. His expression is one of haunted melancholy. He carries a holster and revolver slung from his Sam Browne belt under his greatcoat, which hangs open. The* GERMAN *greets him with quiet satisfaction.* AUNT COLUMBA *slips the tea-cosy over the remaining shell.*]

TAUSCH: *Ach*, so!

SOLDIER: Good evening.

BLAKE: Go away! You're here too soon.

SOLDIER: Well?

TAUSCH: All is well.

BLAKE: Oh, come on in, Lanigan, you grater of verdigris, and be damned to you.

TAUSCH: Commandant, I am so happy that you have arrived in time to prevent any foolishness.

LANIGAN: That's all right.

BLAKE: Herr Tausch – Commandant Lanigan. Have a drink, Belisarius?

LANIGAN: You know I don't touch it.

BLAKE: Still in the same old craw-thumping Band of Hope, eh? And brought them with you too, from all accounts.

LANIGAN: The Works are safe, Herr Tausch. All necessary steps have been taken.

TAUSCH: I am sure.

[*The* AUNT *proceeds to go out.*]

LANIGAN: I'm sorry, but you can't leave here.

AUNT *in* [LANIGAN'S *face as she passes*]: Scum!

AUNT: Stop me! Stop me if you dare! [*She marches out carrying the tray with the hidden shell.*]

TAUSCH: Commandant, I am more than grateful. But I would like to say, now that it is all over, that we have all been the best of friends, and that I will make no charge.

LANIGAN: No charge?

TAUSCH: Let bygones be bygones. Eh, Mr Blake?

BLAKE: Well, well – going to win our hearts by kindness!

TAUSCH: That is not my intention. I said, Mr Blake, that we had all been good friends, and I mean it. That is all.

BLAKE: Most affecting. Well, Belisarius?

TAUSCH: You know each other, I see.

BLAKE: Know Belisarius? Why it was I brought him into the movement in the old days, when we were all one against the British. And now behold my handiwork! The noble, the excellent Free State!

LANIGAN: You're always at me, Blake, but you've more respect for me than you pretend.

BLAKE: The greatest respect. Don't you carry a gun? [*To* BLANAID]: My dear, once upon a time there was an ass laden with sacred relics. 'Behold,' said the ass to himself, 'how all the people kneel down as I pass by. O noble ass! O excellent ass!'

LANIGAN [*darkly*]: All right, Blake.

BLAKE: Come, come. Give Frankenstein his due. [WILLIE *enters.*] So there you are! Where the hell did you go when you were supposed to be on guard?

WILLIE [*indignantly*]: Didn't you hear my mother send me on a message. The Staters out there say they have me under arrest.

BLAKE: Well?

WILLIE: Well yourself!

TAUSCH: It is all right, Willie. You go home quietly. I arrange that nothing more will be said.

WILLIE: Go home? But what about the Works?

TAUSCH: We will say no more about it.

WILLIE: But do they not go up?

TAUSCH: No, Willie.

WILLIE: You called in the Staters?

TAUSCH [*a little crossly*]: That is so.

WILLIE: But that's might against right.

TAUSCH: Well, if you wish to put it that way.

BLAKE: Thus spake Zarathustra.

WILLIE: Oh, that's a terrible thing. Might against right. That's not playing the game, you know.

TAUSCH: That is not a game to me, Willie. It is my business. I have a right to defend myself.

WILLIE: And what about my oath?

[TAUSCH *shrugs his shoulders.*]

WILLIE: Oh, yev tricked us! Without force, says he. Force or unfair influence! Didn't you hear him? And then he calls up the Staters when my back is turned. Oh, there's a thing. But the people of this country can't be cowed by threats.

BLAKE: Oh yes, they can, Willie. Every time. But I'll tell you the right answer to these people. Lanigan can stop us from touching the place to-night. He can lock you and me up if he likes, and in spite of the Bosch. But he can't lock us up for ever. And so long as there's the will in our hearts and the likes of him can only pollute as much of this earth as the area of their own boot soles, so long will the future be before us.

WILLIE: That's right. Up the rebels!

BLAKE: Any answer to that, Belisarius?

LANIGAN: No. I don't think so. As far as it goes.

TAUSCH: Oh, but come, Mr Blake. I would have expected

better of you. I thought that we were friends – that our differences were all fixed up.

BLAKE: Herr Tausch, do you seriously think that our differences can be fixed up by calling in this pretentious gawm. Excuse me while I laugh!

TAUSCH: I bear you no grudge, I assure you.

BLAKE: Nor I you until now. But now no words of mine can express my disappointment in you. And after such an interesting discussion!

[*He laughs in spite of himself.*]

TAUSCH: But what is this? I protest, sir! What right have you to discuss so calmly whether you will blow up my Works? They are mine. I have a right to take steps.

BLAKE: Very well. The next time I call, Herr Tausch, we will dispense with the discussion. I shall have nothing more to say to you.

TAUSCH: But I, sir, will have a great deal to say to you.

BLAKE: Please. The matter is closed.

TAUSCH: It is not closed, Mr Blake, if you respond to my overtures of friendship in this manner.

LANIGAN: Mr Tausch, I suppose that security for these Works is essential?

TAUSCH: Essential! Of course it is essential. I do not understand such a question.

[LANIGAN *nods to himself and starts to put* BLANAID *quietly out of the room.*]

BLAKE: Do I see a piano? Well, well. Would anybody be entertained if I were to render the Chinese National Anthem? Those in favour indicate in the usual way.

[BLAKE *commences to play the Introduction.*]

TAUSCH: The Chinese –! *Lieber Gott!* I will not be treated like this. I refuse to listen. [*Then quietly.*] *Ach*, so. I understand. You make a joke of me. I am the fool of the family! I should have known better than to respond. It is how I have been treated ever since I have come to this place. But I will not be deceived again. Here you will talk a lot, but it comes to nothing. You and your guns that will never fire. I will not be put out again.

BLAKE [*singing*]:
> Fu-I loved the green hills
> And the white clouds.
> Alas he died of drink.

TAUSCH: You will discuss this and that, but I am the only one who will ever *do* anything in this place. Mr Blake, it does not matter to me whether you are in gaol or not, because you can sing songs and make speeches as well in gaol as out of it. And always to the same effect!

BLAKE [*as he plays*]: Oh, Willie. Next parade will be the day I come out. And do see that the stuff is not damp the next time.

[*Singing next verse*]:
> And Li-Po
> Also died drunk.
> He tried to embrace a Moon
> In the Yellow River.

TAUSCH: This is no country! It is a damned Debating Society! Everybody will talk – talk – talk –

BLAKE [*rising after a flourish of chords*]: Died drunk! A pleasing thought. But needing a Nero to do it justice. *Qualis Artifex pereo.*

TAUSCH: But nothing ever happens.

[LANIGAN *without any demonstration shoots* BLAKE *dead. The latter falls with a little sigh of surprise. Then* LANIGAN *slowly puts up his revolver as* BLANAID *appears again in the door and the heads of* GEORGE *and* POTTS *are stuck out of the side door. All are turned to stone.* TAUSCH *springs forward and makes a brief examination.* LANIGAN *turns and walks slowly out, all eyes following him. Then* TAUSCH, *with a sharp intake of breath, rises, bows slightly, and follows him swiftly out. The four other men look on, and, crossing to the*

door, *they stare out after the pair of them with some excitement.*
BLANAID *alone stares at the body on the floor with wide eyes.*]
BLANAID [*coming forward*]: Oh!
[*She sinks down as the men continue to gaze out the door.*]

SLOW CURTAIN

ACT THREE

The Scene is the same as Act One. Several hours have elapsed since the conclusion of the previous Act. The hall door is open and the curtains on the window are drawn. The supper things are still on the table and amongst them is the tea-tray from the Armoury upon which stands the last shell concealed under the tea-cosy. The picture taken from the Armoury is leaning against the wall.

[POTTS *is standing in the open doorway peering out. Presently the model train emerges, and runs round the tracks.* AUNT COLUMBA *appears at the head of the stairs and comes down. She is wearing a hat but no coat.*]

AUNT: Somebody has taken my coat from my bedroom. No-body has any right to touch my things. Nothing is safe in this house. [*She looks around for it and then goes upstairs again, pausing for a moment on the landing.*] You needn't think I don't know where you are.

[DOBELLE *appears from behind the railway and presently he speaks.*]

DOBELLE: Well, can you see what's happening?

POTTS [*gloomily*]: It's gone.

DOBELLE: What? The lorries?

POTTS: Naw. Only one of 'em. Gun's gone.

DOBELLE: But Lanigan?

POTTS: Oh 'im? 'E's still down there postin' guards. 'Orrible fightin' and arguin' there's been.

DOBELLE: What do you mean?

POTTS: That furrin chap. Gone balmy, I guess. Seems to expec' the Commandant to arrest hisself or somethin'. [*He spits.*] It's beyond me.

DOBELLE: I see.

POTTS: Pity about that gun.

DOBELLE [*returning to his train*]: Well, there's nothing to be done, I suppose.

POTTS: Other lorry's still outside. They'll be in 'ere before they go, I guess.

[AUNT COLUMBA *appears once more, this time carrying her coat. She comes down.*]

AUNT: Oh well, if it wasn't touched this time that won't save it the next. I shall have to put a new lock on my door, I can see. All the keys in this house open all the doors. Oh, Captain Potts, please tell George I want to see him before I go. [POTTS *wanders off*.] What time is it? It must be very late. [*She goes and searches the drawers.*] Those are my roller skates, I do believe! How did . . . ? No they're not. I hope people will kindly remember that I have a championship to defend, and if anyone interferes with my skates I won't be answerable for the consequences. Some people don't seem to realize that skating may mean a lot to others.

[*She continues her search. The train runs round and stops in the station. She closes the hall door.*]

DOBELLE [*to the world in general*]: A most peculiar thing! I had quite forgotten the incident, it's so many years ago. I was driving with my uncle in one of those old-fashioned high dog-carts. We were coming back from duck-shooting and a rabbit ran across the road directly in front of us. I remember it distinctly now. My uncle rose from his seat, took a careful aim, and shot the horse through the head. It was a most surprising incident at the time.

[AUNT COLUMBA *stops her searching and presently she crosses quietly behind him.*]

AUNT: Roddy! [*She touches his arm.*]

DOBELLE: Eh – what?

AUNT: I am going away.

DOBELLE: Away. At this hour? Don't be ridiculous, Columba.

AUNT: I can't stay here any longer.

DOBELLE: Where will you go?

AUNT: That doesn't concern you. I shall catch the first train and put my bike in the van.

DOBELLE: Well, you know your own mind best.

AUNT: Roddy, I wish you'd try sometimes to understand my point of view.

DOBELLE: God forbid. I daresay if I understood it, you'd have ruined my life long ago as successfully as you ruined Captain Dopping's.

AUNT: I didn't ruin his life. His own dishonesty was quite sufficient to do that.

DOBELLE: Didn't you keep writing him offensive postcards to the Mess until he was forced to resign from the regiment?

AUNT: I was only asking for what any gentleman would have returned without question – the mowing-machine I gave him. When an engagement is broken off I say it's dishonest not to return the presents.

DOBELLE: I don't suppose the poor fellow had it to return. He had no accommodation for mowing-machines. It was a damn silly present to give him anyway. But what's the use of arguing? I don't want to hurt your feelings, and, besides, I'm tired.

AUNT: Well, why don't you go to bed?

DOBELLE: I don't want to go to bed. I have been spending the night reading the *Inferno* and it has upset me.

AUNT [*goes upstairs*]: Well, I think you ought to go to bed. [*She vanishes into her room and soon reappears with her bicycle.*]

DOBELLE: Columba, have you ever heard of Antenora?

AUNT: No. What's that?

DOBELLE: It's the Hell specially made for traitors to one's country. Have you any idea why Ruggieri, the Archbishop of Pisa, should be placed there, while Rahab, the harlot who betrayed Jericho, goes to Paradise?

AUNT: I'm sure there's a very good reason for it.

DOBELLE: It must have been a little difficult to know where one stood.

AUNT [*fixing her attaché case in her basket*]: Well, talking of Inferno, there is one thing that really makes me uneasy about going away. That child. Roddy, why don't you try and be ni certo her? Just for a little.

DOBELLE: Please, Columba!

AUNT: It's not much to ask of you. And you're not naturally a cruel person.

DOBELLE: I can't see how I'm being cruel to her.

AUNT: Of course you are. She sees nobody. She knows nothing. And she's just at the age when she needs companionship. She used to say her only friend was that Darrell Blake.

DOBELLE: God knows I don't want to make her life a misery. But I can't see what it has got to do with me. How can I do anything for her?

AUNT: You can send her to school.

DOBELLE: To school! To be taught lies and sophistries! To have illegal operations performed upon all her natural instincts. No, Columba! I'm not quite so cruel as that.

AUNT: But she must be educated somehow. I do my best, but you tie my hands so.

DOBELLE: Another convent, I suppose, is indicated. Perhaps even one on the Danube near Pressburg?

AUNT: There you go again. I know you're against religion, Roddy, but remember they only did what was right by Mary and the child according to their lights.

DOBELLE: I'm not against their religion. I am against their rightness. It is right that a woman should die so that a child's immortal soul should be saved from Limbo, therefore I say that I am against right. It is right that men should murder each other for the safety of progress. I admit it. That is why I am against right and believe in wrong. When I look back over my life it's as plain as a pikestaff to me. It is always

Evil that seems to have made life worth while and always Righteousness that has blasted it. And now I solemnly say that I believe in Wrong. I believe in Evil and in Pain and in Decay and, above all, in the Misery that makes Man so much greater than the Angels.

AUNT: Maybe you'll have ample experience of it before you're finished.

DOBELLE: Well, what do you offer me instead? A Paradise where I shall be expected to applaud the torment of my friends – who knows, perhaps even of Mary. Keep it. I prefer to be damned.

AUNT: Mary was a good woman, Roddy. You've no right to talk like that.

DOBELLE: Who can tell? [*There is a knock at the door.*] But here we are arguing again. You'd better go. I don't blame you. Come back when you feel better, and I'll do my best by the child in the meantime.

[*He starts the train and follows it out of sight. She stands in thought until the knock is repeated. She goes to the door and peers out.* GEORGE *and* POTTS *are there. They have lost much of their buoyancy.*]

AUNT [*letting them in*]: Oh, it's you, is it? Been drowning your troubles in drink, I suppose, as usual.

GEORGE: No, but we've been giving them a damn good swimming lesson. Potts says you want to see me.

AUNT: Yes, come in. I have something to show you. Where are the others?

GEORGE: You mean Lanigan and the Bosch? Oh, down below. That German is off his rocker, you know. These foreigners! Anything knocks them over.

AUNT: Why, what's he doing?

GEORGE: Oh, going around. It's been a terrible night. And as if he hadn't done enough already, he's marching round objecting to everything. I declare to God I'd hate to be Lanigan out to-night with that fellow on the loose.

AUNT: Nonsense. They're hand in glove.

POTTS: Could I have ... glass of water, please ... voice gone.

[*She indicates the carafe and he drinks.*]

GEORGE: First we carried poor Darry up to the Isolation Hospital. And then we came back and tried to reason with those fellows about the gun. It was no good, though. They took it off in one of the lorries. Poor Potts is terribly cut up. On such a day too.

AUNT: And Willie?

GEORGE: Oh, a very bad business. They took him off in the lorry as well. He was raving and swearing that he's going to get Lanigan. You wouldn't believe it was the same fellow. Seeing red.

AUNT: Well, what would you expect?

GEORGE: It's been a terrible night.

AUNT: Terrible. But not so terrible as it might have been. George, I've saved something for you.

GEORGE: Saved something for me?

AUNT: Yes. Trust a woman to be the only one to keep her head in a crisis. If it wasn't for me you'd have nothing left. Look.

[*She proceeds to raise the tea-cosy. There is a knock at the door and she replaces it.*]

AUNT: What do you suppose that was?

GEORGE: Somebody wants to come in.

AUNT: Well, open it and see.

GEORGE: Me?

AUNT: Yes, go on.

GEORGE: Hadn't you better? It's your house.

AUNT: I will not. You're a man, or supposed to be one.

TAUSCH [*off*]: Aal-lo!

GEORGE: It's the Bosch! Good God, what do you suppose he's up to now?

TAUSCH [*off*]: Open, please.

[GEORGE *opens the door and* TAUSCH *and* LANIGAN *enter.*]

GEORGE: Both of them!

[*They all stand looking at one another for some seconds.*]

LANIGAN: Is Mr Dobelle about?

DOBELLE [*appearing*]: You want me?

LANIGAN: I'm going now. I've told the men at the gate to let nobody through but the lighthouse-men and anyone you give one of these passes to.

[*He sits at the table and commences to write.*]

DOBELLE: I see. How long must we have a guard?

LANIGAN: That depends upon Headquarters.

TAUSCH: Commandant Lanigan, how often must I repeat that I do not wish to have either you or your men in my Works. I do not require the type of protection you provide, and I will not have myself associated with you in the eyes of the public.

LANIGAN: I've told you already we're here to stay whether you like it or not. These Works are a National affair.

TAUSCH: And to the Nation I will answer for them. They are in no danger now except from your presence.

LANIGAN [*to* DOBELLE]: I'm leaving you half a dozen in blank. You must fill in the names of your tradesmen and visitors for yourself. I suppose six will be enough?

DOBELLE: I think so.

TAUSCH: Furthermore, I insist upon knowing whether you intend to surrender yourself to the law. It seems to me the most dignified course for you to take in the circumstances, and it will save me the painful necessity of having you arrested. If you will not give me your honourable undertaking then I must assume the worst of your intentions.

LANIGAN: Ah, will you leave me alone. Haven't I had enough?

TAUSCH: Mr Dobelle, will you please oblige me with a piece of notepaper and an envelope.

DOBELLE: Try the drawer of the table.

TAUSCH: I thank you.

[*He sits and prepares to write.*]

AUNT: Well, good-bye, Roddy.

DOBELLE: Good-bye.

TAUSCH [*rising politely*]: You are leaving, Miss Dobelle?

AUNT: I have nothing to say to you.

TAUSCH: To me?

AUNT: I hope for your own peace of mind you have as little conscience as you seem to have. We will not meet again. [*She pushes her bicycle off.*]

TAUSCH: Am I correct in thinking that the lady suggests there is something on *my* conscience?

GEORGE: Well, it was rather dirty work, you know, old man. Willie's right. You tricked those boys into this.

TAUSCH: That is monstrous, sir!

GEORGE: Mind you, I didn't see what happened. I'm no witness. I wasn't in the room at the time. But from what I've heard, it wasn't on the level.

TAUSCH: A crime has been committed. Are you accusing me, sir?

GEORGE: Ah, I don't accuse anyone. But it wasn't straight, you know. Leaves a bad taste in the mouth, old man. No! I'd have expected better. But then, of course – foreigners – you know. Not good sports. [*He shakes his head and, crossing to the table, he sits down silently beside POTTS and sinks into gloomy reflections.*]

TAUSCH: I never heard of such a thing. Even Commandant Lanigan appears to have some grievance against me!

LANIGAN [*rising and buttoning his coat*]: Ah, never mind that. I only said it was you wanted your Works secure.

TAUSCH: I do. But did I ask you to commit a crime? You admit yourself that there is no excuse for what you have done. It is – I can use no other word – it is murder!

DOBELLE: Why not call it War? That's a well-known palliative.

TAUSCH: Pardon me, Mr Dobelle. In war there are certain rules that must be observed.

DOBELLE: I don't see that that's of much importance. From the point of view of the man who dies, it makes very little difference whether he is killed according to rules or not.

LANIGAN: Ah, what's the use of arguing! I was a rebel once. What I've done was War then. Now I'm on the other side and it's murder. I admit it.

DOBELLE: Don't try to explain, Lanigan. Your friends don't want it, and your enemies won't believe you anyhow.

LANIGAN: I'm not trying to explain.

TAUSCH: Well, I must say I admire your frankness, Commandant. But I do not think that it will assist your position when I have made my report to the Attorney-General.

LANIGAN: When I took on this job I said to myself: 'Well, I'll last as long as God allows me.' So make your report and be done with it. If I don't get what's coming to me for this business, I suppose I'll be plugged sooner or later by somebody.

TAUSCH [writing]: You need not be plugged, as you say, by anybody if you do not do these things.

LANIGAN: Somebody has got to do them . . . if the country's to go on.

TAUSCH: That is quite untrue. How can you say such a thing?

LANIGAN: Ah, never mind. I'm a physical-force man born and bred in the movement. I'm only doing my job – the job I'm able to do – the job that always seems to deliver the goods. There's no excuse for it, I daresay. I don't pretend to be clever like he was. He was the brains and inspiration of the movement in the old days against the British. But now we seem to have a damn sight too many brains, and inspiration always ends in trying to blow up something.

TAUSCH: And so you assassinate that inspiration!

LANIGAN: I suppose you think I enjoy that, when it means a bullet in my own back sooner or later. But enjoy it or not, I've always been taught that it's not words but deeds the country needs, and I'll have to go on doing what I can, no matter.

TAUSCH: A very fine attitude for young revolutionaries to adopt, maybe. But you are a man of responsibilities. The State cannot ignore the forms of justice.

LANIGAN: Forms! Do you think Blake wanted a lot of play-acting in Court to find out what everybody knew already? And then they'd have tried to break his heart in gaol in order to put a bit more venom into him for the next attempt.

TAUSCH: Ah! Quite a humanitarian, after all!

LANIGAN: I don't know about that. It was he that always had the wit to find the word for these things. Not me. But I only hope that when my time comes I'll be plugged fair and clean like he was, with none of the tomfoolery of Law and Justice and the torment they call 'Prepare to meet your God!'

TAUSCH: That is all you have to say before I send this letter to the Attorney-General?

LANIGAN: Ah, what more is there to be said? I'm a gunman. I always was and I always will be. And if you ask me why, I declare to God I don't know. There's no glamour on my side, nowadays. But God help you all if I wasn't, is what I say. It may be brains and inspiration that makes the country at the start, but it's my help you're always telephoning for before the end.

TAUSCH: Well, I am amazed!

LANIGAN: There are times when it's best to destroy the things that are nearest to us.

TAUSCH: I have heard that we are supposed to love our enemies in this life. But you would work upon the principle that we must kill our friends, eh?

LANIGAN: If there's any man could answer that, it's the man that has gone. And I believe that if ever I meet him again he'll bear me less ill-will for what's finished and done with, than those that are left behind. So, shot in an attack on the Works, is my report. If you know better – well, I won't blame you for saying so. It'll be all the same, I suppose, for *they'll* get me in the end, if you don't. But, by God, they'll not touch this Power House again! You'll see that I'm right there. Whatever happens now will be a personal matter between me and the likes of Willie Reilly. The Works will be out of it. Good-night, gentlemen. [*He goes. The lorry outside is heard to start.*]

DOBELLE: The Moor has done his work. The Moor may go.

TAUSCH: Mr Dobelle, that man is a scoundrel. But do you think that he is sincere in what he says?

DOBELLE: Maybe you are thinking that there are more ways than one in which a man may die for his country?

TAUSCH: Do you feel like that?

DOBELLE: No. I say, let my country die for me.

TAUSCH: Perhaps it would be best for you to make this report, Mr Dobelle. I would do it, but – I am a stranger. Perhaps –

DOBELLE: Denounce Lanigan, you mean?

TAUSCH: Some person will have to do so, of course.

DOBELLE: There were only three of us there at the time. Willie was committing a felony and can say nothing of any weight. That leaves just you and I.

TAUSCH: I agree. Yes. Just you and me.

DOBELLE: Well, you can rule me out. I don't like the man, but hanging him won't bring back Darrell Blake.

TAUSCH: But murder. It is murder!

DOBELLE: Murder! Yes. The birth of a Nation is no imma- culate conception.

TAUSCH: But your feelings for your friend who is dead?

DOBELLE: He seems to have been Lanigan's friend too. There is no cure for death.

TAUSCH: Do you try to justify this man Lanigan?

DOBELLE: No. Yet when Lanigan dies he will leave behind

him you and your Works. When I die nothing will be left but the squabbling of female connexions.

TAUSCH: *Das heisst* – you admire him, so?

DOBELLE: No, I hate him. Hate him like poison. But if I were to see him hanged, whenever I turned on your light I should feel more sorry for him than for my friend Darrell Blake. And I could not endure that. I prefer to continue hating him. Besides, would any jury accept the testimony of a man like me against Lanigan's? But they'll believe you, Herr Tausch. Oh yes, they'll believe you every time.

[TAUSCH *hesitates and then goes on with his letter.* GEORGE *gathers himself together and raises the tea-cosy.*]

GEORGE: Have some cold tea, Captain? We may as well. Oh!

POTTS: 'Ello! Where cher get that?

GEORGE: The last of the Mohicans. This must be what the old lady said she had saved for us.

POTTS: That was decent of her, George.

GEORGE: Not that it's much good, old man.

TAUSCH: A little give and take. A few words around the table. We were good enemies, Mr Blake and I, and we would have come to understand each other before long.

DOBELLE: You would never have understood Blake. He belonged to a different world that had no chance against yours – a world that must inevitably have been destroyed by you. You remember Li-Po? He was trying to embrace the Moon in the Yellow River.

TAUSCH: But I assure you, I would not think of destroying anything. We would have lived, side by side, in harmony, respecting each other's point of view.

DOBELLE: Never with him. You'd always have been disturbing the waters with your machinery and drowning his moon in mud. No, in the end you would either have had to kill him or to give up your fight. You remember – he who establishes a despotism and slays not Brutus abideth but a little time.

TAUSCH: I wonder why the people whom we can like most easily are always on the wrong side? Why must Mr Blake be against me and Commandant Lanigan be my protector? Why must I have these monstrous doctrines foisted upon my shoulders?

DOBELLE: I told you, there are monsters in the mists that will glare back at you with your own face.

TAUSCH: Why always talk in parables, Mr Dobelle? You seem to wish to make everything appear unreal.

DOBELLE: If there was anything real in your sense of the word about to-night, was it not Lanigan's shot? That should satisfy even your thirst for reality.

TAUSCH: I see what you are at, Mr Dobelle. You wish me to believe that Lanigan's shot was part of my world – that he and I are truly on the same side.

DOBELLE: More than that. Lanigan is just yourself. He is your finger on the trigger. Denounce him by all means. The tribute to your Works is not yet complete. For if he doesn't hang for Blake then Willie will hang for him, and I'm sure you'd like to save Willie. But before you denounce him, I say you must give me an answer to what he has said. And you won't do that. Because there is no answer, and you know it.

TAUSCH: Mr Dobelle, you drive me very far.

DOBELLE: Do you complain of this? What nonsense! Two more lives, Herr Tausch, but what of it! In this welter of blood one great factor will be borne in upon us. The Works will remain. Man may perish, but they have been saved. Hallelujah!

TAUSCH: Enough of this.

DOBELLE: The inspiration that threatened them is no more. Nothing remains but the sordid squabble of Willie and Lanigan, in which the Works will be forgotten and your programme will go through. I surrender, Herr Tausch. You are the victor after all.

TAUSCH: All guilt must be avenged on earth. I am going to send this letter, Mr Dobelle.

DOBELLE: Then why the delays of the post? The telephone is still at your disposal.

TAUSCH [*after a moment's consideration*]: I do not know, sir, whether you regard me as a fool or a lunatic, but whatever may have been the effect of this evening's events upon other people, I, at least, have retained my common sense. I shall be glad to use your telephone.

DOBELLE: Do, sir. For the second time this evening.

[TAUSCH *glares at him for a moment and then crosses to the telephone, and takes up the directory.*]

GEORGE: I say, Potts, let's get rid of the damn thing. It makes me depressed.

POTTS: Same 'ere, George. I'm sick of the sight of it.

GEORGE: What do you say we chuck it away?

POTTS: Where?

GEORGE: Oh, anywhere. Into the sea. I don't want to see it again.

POTTS: What 'appens when the tide goes out?

GEORGE: Well, over the wall on to the old slag heap. Anywhere we'll be rid of it.

POTTS: Just as you say, George.

TAUSCH [*after some consideration, has thrown aside the directory and picked up the receiver*]: Allo.

GEORGE [*rising*]: Well, bring it along, Potts, old man. I'm bloody well fed up.

POTTS [*rising and taking the shell*]: Only good for the slag 'eap, I'm afraid. Oh, we've been badly let down. Eight years' work gone up the spout.

[*They go off leaving the door open, through which the turbines hum merrily. It is a little lighter outside.*]

TAUSCH: Allo. Is that the Exchange? Yes. I want Ballsbridge 586 please. Yes, that is right. No. Never mind. Ring till they answer, please.

DOBELLE: Until we had the telephone we were quite out of touch with civilization. [*Pause.*] Certainly if I were the Attorney-General I'd agree to prosecute anybody at this hour of the morning.

TAUSCH: Pardon. I speak with the German Legation. It is a matter for them what steps are taken.

DOBELLE: Oh, cowardly.

TAUSCH: Mr Dobelle, when I have telephoned I am going away and I do not think that we will meet again – socially. I do not appreciate your satiric neurosis and I do not wish to lose my temper. But do not think, sir, that I have no answer to what you say. What I am doing here is greater than any of the considerations you fling at me – yes, greater even than the life of a man. I am not afraid to say it, even if that life must be my own. What is the life of a man beside the future of humanity? There is a purpose in this life, my dear sir, that transcends all personal feelings. Allo. My dear sir, you have only to go outside and look around you. Everything you see has its purpose in the scheme of things. You stand upon the sea wall and look down at the Works below. What do you see? Allo. Yes. Yes, I wait still. The great river is there – the granite pier – the navigation lock – the turbine house beside the old slag heap. Everything with a purpose.

DOBELLE: Even the slag heap?

TAUSCH: Yes even – allo. Is that the Secretary? This is Tausch speaking. I have a Report for the Minister. Yes, a serious Report.

> [*Outside there is a livid flash and a roar. In a moment it is followed by the sound of falling masonry. Then the lights go out. When silence comes again the sound of the turbines is no more and a red glow illumines the sky behind the parapet.*]

GEORGE [*off*]: Potts! Potts!

POTTS [*off*]: Are you hurt, George?

TAUSCH [*dashing to the door*]: The Works!

GEORGE [*appearing outside*]: It was a good one – a good one, Potts.

POTTS [*far away*]: Bet-cher-life!

TAUSCH: What has happened to the Works?

GEORGE: Pure accident. Sorry, must be off.

[DOBELLE *begins to laugh as he lights a lamp.* TAUSCH *seizes* GEORGE *by the collar.*]

TAUSCH: Come here! Stop!

GEORGE: Oh, a damn good one! Who'd have thought it?

TAUSCH: Is anybody hurt? The night shift! Where are they?

GEORGE: Running like hell, old man. Can't be dead if they run like that.

[DOBELLE *picks up the dangling telephone receiver and speaks into it before replacing it.*]

DOBELLE: Did the Minister get that Report?

[TAUSCH *releases* GEORGE *and dashes to the sea wall, over which he looks before returning. There is distant shouting from outside.* GEORGE *goes.*]

TAUSCH: *Du lieber Gott!*

DOBELLE: You were telling me – about a purpose – a purpose in this life – a purpose . . . [*he laughs quite hysterically*] for the old slag heap!

TAUSCH: Please. Please.

DOBELLE [*lighting a lamp at the table*]: You were explaining to me – your philosophy – excuse me – my satiric neurosis – it overcomes me . . . [*He laughs.*]

TAUSCH: My Works! My Works!

DOBELLE: Your Works! Your memories! Brutus is avenged, O Octavius.

TAUSCH: Isn't it enough that a man has died and that my plant has been destroyed? Must we have laughter and jeers as well?

DOBELLE: It is not I – it is this Land – this Life. Take your Works where they belong. Here is Hesperides – the Garden where men may sleep.

TAUSCH: I think I go mad! . . . [*The shouting outside resumes.*] But I forget. Somebody may be injured. I must not give way. I will go down and search in the ruins. I must go at once.

[*He goes. The red glow in the court is streaked with the first sunlight.* DOBELLE *closes the door behind him as if to shut it all out.*]

DOBELLE: Yes, be off . . . search in the ruins. Search them well. Turn the scorched sod over. It will be all the same in the end. You'll never learn anything, and I'll never do anything. There's no end and there's no solution. [*He picks up the picture of his wife.*] Ah, Mary, have pity on me and on poor Tausch. No, not on Tausch. He's too great to need pity. But me . . . Ah, Bice – *la dolce guida* . . . take away this cursed gift of laughter and give us tears instead.

[*At the head of the stairs is a white figure. He sees it with a gasp.*]

DOBELLE: Mary!

BLANAID: I'm frightened.

DOBELLE: Your voice! Why are you standing there looking at me, Mary?

BLANAID: Don't you know me, Father? [*She comes down.*]

DOBELLE: Know you! Why – what am I saying?

BLANAID: I saw a glare and then there was a terrible bang. Aren't you well?

DOBELLE: It's Blanaid! I didn't recognize you. You're so changed, child. You seem to have grown up suddenly.

BLANAID: I am not changed. Only you hardly ever look at me.

DOBELLE: I believe I don't. I wonder why. Stay with me for a little.

BLANAID: I was hoping you'd let me. In case there's another bang.

DOBELLE: There won't. It's all over now. [*Offering her a chair*]: Won't you sit down?

D

BLANAID: Thank you kindly.

DOBELLE [*sitting too*]: I wonder what is the proper way to begin on meeting one's daughter for the first time?

BLANAID: I should say, 'Are you staying long in these parts?'

DOBELLE: I rather hope you are.

BLANAID [*kneeling beside him*]: Daddy, why do you never talk to me? Why do you hate me so?

DOBELLE: Because – because I'm an old fool. Because I thought that life had played its last trick on me. [*The lamp flickers.*] I'm afraid there's not much oil in that lamp.

BLANAID: Did I take her from you? [*He smiles.*] I'm sorry.

DOBELLE: I remember. That lock of hair used to do that.

BLANAID: When I grow up I'm going to try to be like her. I think I can. A Guide never gives up. Daddy.

DOBELLE: Yes, my dear.

BLANAID: Will you take my education in hand from now on?

DOBELLE: In what way?

BLANAID: I thought perhaps I might ask you questions from time to time.

DOBELLE: I'll do my best. If they're not too difficult.

BLANAID: Only from time to time, you know.

DOBELLE: Whenever you like.

BLANAID: May I ask one now?

DOBELLE: Well, only one. Then you must go to sleep and rest yourself. Well, what is it?

BLANAID: Do you know why people aren't happy?

[*There is a pause, during which she settles down and goes to sleep without really waiting for an answer. Through the cracks in the shutters the morning starts to shine.*]

DOBELLE: Well, I think that puts an end to my part in your education. I wonder, after all, do they want to be happy? The trees don't bother and they're not unhappy. And the flowers too. It's only men who are different, and it's only men who can be really unhappy. And yet isn't it unhappiness that makes men so much greater than the trees and the

flowers and all the other things that can't feel as we do?
I used to thank the Devil for that and call him my friend.
But there's more to it than that. I suppose the Devil can do
nothing for us until God gives him a chance. Or maybe it's
because they're both the same person. Those glittering
sorrows, eh? Asleep? Well, here endeth the first lesson.
[*Pause, while the lamp sinks lower and his head nods.*] Darkness . . . Death and Darkness. Ah, can anything cure them?
. . . I wonder.

> [*He closes his eyes. Presently* AGNES *opens the hall door and
> comes in. It is morning outside and the sunlight floods into the
> room from behind her. She crosses to the window and opens the
> shutters with a sigh of intense satisfaction and smiles out at the
> flowers and the ivy that grow around the frame. Nodding her
> head, and with an approving click of her tongue, she softly
> hums a lullaby and surveys a new day. A ship hoots in the
> river. That is the end of this Play.*]

CURTAIN

JOSEPH O'CONOR

The Iron Harp

The harp of the Harper of Finn had three strings: the bronze, which put the listeners to sleep; the silver, which put them to laughter; and the iron, which put them to tears.

Applications for permission to perform this play by professionals must be made to Margaret Ramsay Ltd, 14a Goodwin's Court, London WC2. No performance may take place unless a licence has first been obtained.

THE IRON HARP

This play was first presented at the Guildford Repertory Theatre on 21 November 1955, with the following cast:

PETER TOLLY	John Moore
SHAMUS	Eric Jones
MICHAEL O'RIORDON	Joseph O'Conor
MOLLY KINSELLA	Linda Dixon
CAPTAIN JOHN TREGARTHEN	Dennis Chinnery
SEAN KELLY	Diarmuid Kelly
SCANLON	Henry Manning
1ST BLACK AND TAN SOLDIER	Hubert Forde
2ND BLACK AND TAN SOLDIER	Roger Ostime
DERMOT	Edward Kelsey
PHELIM	Allan Barnes

Produced by David William

The Iron Harp won the Charles Henry Foyle New Play Award for 1955–6

CHARACTERS

PETER TOLLY, *an Englishman with property in Ireland*

SHAMUS, *a retainer*

MICHAEL O'RIORDON, *in Tolly's employ, also an officer in the I.R.A.*

MOLLY KINSELLA, *cousin to Michael*

CAPTAIN JOHN TREGARTHEN, *a British Army Officer, prisoner in Michael's charge*

SEAN KELLY, *a high officer in the I.R.A.*

SCANLON, *his aide*

1ST BLACK AND TAN SOLDIER

2ND BLACK AND TAN SOLDIER

DERMOT, *I.R.A. Sentry*

PHELIM, *I.R.A. Sentry*

SCENE:

Lounge-hall of an Irish Mansion, owned by an Englishman, Peter Tolly

TIME: *April 1920*

ACT ONE	*Morning*
ACT TWO	*The same day – afternoon*
ACT THREE	*The next morning, about 5.30*

ACT ONE

Lounge-hall of an Irish mansion owned by an Englishman, PETER TOLLY, *heir to the fortune of a sanitary engineer. Somewhat mouldering grandeur: silver candlesticks, oil ancestors, fine glass, disrepair. Door to drive and grounds, staircase visible, the long windows are heavily curtained so the stage is gloomy though daylight filters.*

[*In an alcove out of sight of the stairs, his face away from the audience, sits* MICHAEL O'RIORDON, *recently blinded. In the distance a train whistles three times.*]

TOLLY [*coming downstairs*]: I told you so: the train already.

SHAMUS: Don't ye be fretting now. Didn't I tell Tim at the station ye were coming? He'll wait. Anyway like as not he'll yarn with Dan the driver till an hour from now.

TOLLY: Well hurry, please: I must be in London by to-morrow.

SHAMUS [*moving with enormous slowness*]: Time enough, sorr, time enough. Life must be lived like a slow dance, y'know. A ritual, that's what it is, a ritual. You wouldn't expect to see Father O'Sullivan *scamper* up the steps to the altar, now would ye? [*Dumps bags at bottom of stairs and turns to go up.*] Now suppose these here were the altar steps: ye turn slow, and ye lift your foot ceremonial and careful as a giant crossing the Causeway –

TOLLY: Use your imagination some other way, please. Any way so long as you're quick. Really, you haven't drawn the curtains yet and it's past ten o'clock. What do you do with yourself until now?

SHAMUS: Well, sorr, I rose at six-thirty, just as the sun looked through me curtains, and addressed meself first to –

TOLLY: All right, all right, I'm sorry I asked! I'll do this. [*He opens the curtains.*] People will think someone's died. [*Two shots in the distance.*] Oh, dear Heaven, don't say there's more trouble.

SHAMUS: Now, if you'd only listen slowly with all your both ears, you'd know that couldn't be trouble. It's only a little 22 gun for shooting rabbits, not a big 303 gun for shooting Englishmen – God love ye sorr, I forgot you was one yourself. No ill-will, now, no ill-will at all.

TOLLY: Peace and quiet, that's the only reason I bought this house; now you can't put your head out of the window without being shot at.

SHAMUS: It's only rabbits is in any jeopardy, now, sorr, so maybe you're safe. [*Quickly*]: It'll be the young Captain Johnny, with Miss Molly, I shouldn't wonder. Sure, they're often out these days shooting.

TOLLY: Perhaps someone will deign to tell me before I go who this Captain Johnny is and what he's doing here. I come back for a few days and find my house infested by natives with guns, and one strange Captain of the British Army who spends his time shooting rabbits. I just don't understand it all.

SHAMUS: Ah now, 'native' is a terrible derogatory thing to say about an Irishman.

TOLLY: We're all natives, that's the penalty of being born.

SHAMUS: Is that it? But didn't Mr Michael tell you about Captain Johnny?

TOLLY: I have not exchanged two words with O'Riordon since I came: he's never here. I employ the man to run my estate, and he acts as though the house belonged to him. I presume they're his friends who clutter my corridors? Where is he now? I must have a word with him before I go.

O'RIORDON [*from the wingchair*]: For God's sake, are *you* blind as well?

TOLLY: Oh dear, what a start you gave me. Well, there you

are anyway. Shamus, where is Mick with the trap? You can be getting these bags on board.

SHAMUS: Mick's sick. I'll just go and harness it meself.

TOLLY: Sick! Not harnessed yet! We'll never make that train.

SHAMUS: Oh yes we will, sorr: they'll be playing poker at the station as like as not.

[*Exit.*]

TOLLY: Well, O'Riordon – ?

O'RIORDON: Well, Tolly boy?

TOLLY: I'm hoping before I go for some explanation.

O'RIORDON: Of what?

TOLLY: Of why my house has been turned into a barracks, who these men are who walk in and out of my property, and who is this mysterious English Captain? Dare I hope for some light?

O'RIORDON: Dare you hope for some light? That's asking a lot. But I'll answer your questions. First, Captain John Tregarthen is an officer of the British Army and is my prisoner.

TOLLY: Your – ?

O'RIORDON: He was captured near Dublin three months ago, and was sent up here in my charge. For reasons that should be clear even to yourself, I can't watch him, nor can we spare men to guard him. So he's on parole and at the moment shooting rabbits.

TOLLY: Oh, I see.

O'RIORDON: Lucky you!

TOLLY: But O'Riordon, there is one fact that seems to have eluded you: this is my house, you work for me, I pay your wages. Therefore, it is I who say who comes here and who does not. What is more, I am an Englishman and will not allow a British Army officer to be held prisoner here. Why, if it was ever known in London I should be arrested – as a traitor perhaps. Why can't you think of other people for a change?

O'RIORDON: Stop talking to yourself, Tolly boy. You can tell the police in London if you wish that your house has been requisitioned by the Irish Army: I don't suppose they'll take any notice of you. And you can tell Captain Tregarthen, if you care to, that he is free to go: but I don't think *he* will take any notice of you. AND now, here am I taking no notice of you either. It's an indifferent world, Tolly, and it's no lie.

TOLLY: Now, I've been very tolerant.

O'RIORDON: Tolly the Tolerant –

TOLLY: No one can say I've not been. Can you? But this must stop. I'm not a politician, I'm just a business man, and I've closed my eyes to a great deal. But at least I expect you to be polite. You seem to forget I can dismiss you. You mustn't presume, you know, just because –

O'RIORDON: Now, don't throw your pennyworth of pity in the blind man's hat. You don't keep me because you're sorry for me, you keep me because I do your work for you here and do it well: your little estate is efficiently worked for you and cosily kept for you, so that you can scuttle here for a quiet time when you've exhausted your spirit selling lavatory-pans to the world.

TOLLY: There's no need to sneer. My business is a very necessary one.

O'RIORDON: Yes, yes, you're a hygienic fellow and no one's denying it: perhaps that's why you're out of place here. Do you know what's happening in Ireland? Your beneficent Government has sent over here the scum of your prisons, armed to the teeth, to kill the likes of me. Have you ever heard of the Black-and-Tans? Or are the English newspapers ashamed to mention them? They're the gentry who ambushed my patrol six months ago, and since then it doesn't matter where I face in a room: there are no windows anywhere. So you'll forgive me, Tolly boy, if I don't seem sympathetic when you protest at the presence of my

friends here. I know it's your house, but it's also a con-
venient headquarters, so here we stay.

TOLLY: But how long is this going on? You must see what
an embarrassment this is for me. I do sympathize, of course—

O'RIORDON: Well, thank you for that. And it'll go on, I
suppose, until Ireland is independent. Then God knows
what we'll do with ourselves! If it's any happiness to you,
the British regulars I've met are nearly as angry about the
Tans as we are: Captain Johnny spits whenever they're
mentioned.

TOLLY: Well, I just don't understand and won't try to, what's
more. And I can't wait to get back to London. I'm only
sorry I came.

O'RIORDON: Don't believe yourself, man. When you get
back you'll boast your head off. [*A shot in the distance.*]
Don't worry, 'tis only the rabbits. Look out of the window,
now, and tell me if there's a big fellow in the drive, talking
maybe to a lad with black hair.

TOLLY [*looking out*]: They're both there, yes.

O'RIORDON: Well, the big fellow is Sean Kelly. He's just
arrived. He fought the Germans at Mons, was wounded
and discharged. He then came over to Dublin, fought with
me against the English in the Easter trouble of '16, was condemned to death and reprieved to go back and fight in
France. He finished with the British Army last year, fighting the Russians. Now here he is, back in Ireland. He's that
rare eagle, a soldier of fortune, and one of the great ones.
When you're an old man, Tolly boy, and your grandsons
– if you're so lucky as to have them – around your knees,
you'll have some golden memories pouched in your old
leather head. 'Boys,' you can say, 'at my mansion in Ireland stayed Sean Kelly himself.' And they'll think to themselves: 'He may not look much now, but beGod when he
was young he walked with heroes!'

TOLLY: No, I'm afraid I could never be mistaken for a hero,

even by grandsons. And to prove my point I shall leave post-haste. Thank goodness we're not far from the border. When I'm in Belfast I shall breathe again.

O'RIORDON: That's where we differ. When I'm in Belfast I stop breathing.

[*Enter* SHAMUS.]

SHAMUS: There we are, sorr. A record for a swift ceremonious harnessing. Tim'll be holding the train, so don't you fret.

TOLLY: I'm afraid I don't trust Tim. He'll be dead drunk, as like as not.

SHAMUS: Well, sorr, that's as it should be. At our age, things should be accustomed, y'know. So when Tim visits me here, he knows what to expect: here's meself, busy about your business. And when I visit Tim, I knows what to expect too: there's himself, plastered.

[*Exit* SHAMUS *with bags.*]

TOLLY [*shaking* O'RIORDON'S *hand*]: Good-bye, O'Riordon.

[*Enter* MOLLY KINSELLA.]

MOLLY: Hello, Mr Tolly, are you off so soon?

TOLLY: Oh yes! And I can't say I'm sorry. I came here for peace and quiet.

MOLLY: What an odd thing to do!

TOLLY: Now I must fly before your cousin Michael converts me, and I find myself fighting for Ireland.

MOLLY: Mr Tolly, what a good idea. I can teach you to shoot.

TOLLY: Good-bye!

[*Exit.*]

SHAMUS [*off*]: The horse is pawing the earth, sorr, and all's ready for the ride.

TOLLY [*off*]: Dear me, is this trap safe?

MOLLY: Poor Tolly, with his umbrella and his bowler: he didn't know what he was coming into. We should have put a shot through his hat so that he could show his clients at home.

O'RIORDON: It's not too late. Try a shot from the door.

MOLLY: Ah no, he's suffered enough. He may not reach the station alive, anyway; Shamus is a terror with the trap.

O'RIORDON: He's a good feller, Tolly, but he always brings out the bully in me. As soon as I hear him I reach for the nearest insult.

MOLLY: I always feel such a fool when I see him: 'Good morning, Molly.' 'Good morning, Tolly,' like some terrible cross-talk act.

O'RIORDON: We might make up a fine jingly ballad out of that.

MOLLY: And you could sing it to him when he next comes.

O'RIORDON: Yes, I'll get it ready. [*Tentatively sings to 'The Green Bushes':*] 'O, Tolly met Molly one fine day in spring' –

MOLLY: Any tea on the hob?

O'RIORDON: Shamus will have left some.

[MOLLY *goes off.*]

O'RIORDON [*singing*]: 'Says Tolly to Molly, I'm the lavatory King.' I wonder why no one ever calls him by his Christian name.

MOLLY [*off*]: Who?

O'RIORDON: Tolly.

MOLLY: Maybe he's not a Christian.

O'RIORDON: Or maybe it's worse than his surname. God help him. [*Sings*]: 'Says Molly to Tolly, "Will you leave me alone?"'

MOLLY [*entering*]: Have a cup yourself?

O'RIORDON: Thanks, I will. [*Sings*]: 'The place for a King is a-sitting on his throne.' Sorry. Where have you been this morning?

MOLLY: Out riding.

O'RIORDON: By yourself? Why didn't you tell me? I'd have liked a ride.

MOLLY: Oh, Rory's gone lame, and I know you like to ride him these days.

O'RIORDON: Ah, sure I'll take a risk on any of them. What does it matter?

MOLLY: Anyway, Johnny came so I wasn't alone.

O'RIORDON: Oh, I thought I heard him out shooting rabbits.

MOLLY: We both were, but we thought it would be fun from horseback for a change.

O'RIORDON: God help you. Did you hit anything?

MOLLY: No rabbits, but I winged a tree.

O'RIORDON: Where's Johnny now?

MOLLY: Seeing to the horses. He won't be long.

O'RIORDON: You know, I have to talk to myself severely at times and tell myself he's my prisoner. I don't know, even so, that I believe it. The world in my head's not the same as it was: I see by another light entirely, and some things and people look altogether more beautiful. Friends do. Is he an English officer at all, or just a dear friend? God's compensating gift to the blind? Which is he?

MOLLY: Both.

O'RIORDON: Yes. You know, I've often wondered what he's like: the first friend I've had since – these last six months. I wonder now if he's as fine as I see him in my head. Describe him, come on.

MOLLY: No, no, Michael.

O'RIORDON: Come on, you and I have always liked the same people, so you'll describe him just as I'd see him myself.

MOLLY: You've a fine picture there in your head, and that's just about what he looks like.

O'RIORDON: Does he now. That's lovely. But it's queer, all the same. There are the rest of my friends, hung round the inside of my skull like a portrait gallery in a dark tower. But Johnny's a voice outside, or a footstep, or a rifle shot maybe, in the distance.

MOLLY: Well, it's good to know you love him. If every enemy were like you, Michael, this old war wouldn't last a frown longer. Another cup?

O'RIORDON: No thanks. And I hope you realize, my girl, how lucky *you* are: you'll stay in my mind for ever young, as lovely as you are this April day. Anyone who's a friend of mine lives in Tir-nan-Og. Isn't that a fine gift, now, for your next birthday?

MOLLY: Oh, must I wait till then? Can't I have it now?

O'RIORDON: As an *un*birthday present, you mean?

MOLLY: Yes. D'you remember how many of those you gave me when I was a kid and couldn't bear to wait a year?

O'RIORDON: I do indeed, But I didn't mind. Sure, giving and taking's both grand fun. Well, here's your present – perpetual youth.

MOLLY: Oh, thank you, kind sir.

O'RIORDON: Sad, is it not, that we seem more beautiful the less light there is.

MOLLY: Oh, come now.

O'RIORDON: No, by sunlight the best of us can look a bit haggard. By candlelight we're all half-enchanted, and by the light of a darkness the like of mine we're gods and goddesses itself. What do you make of it? Riddle me that one.

MOLLY: So, Michael. Is every girl you meet a goddess?

O'RIORDON: For God's sake, no! There's many a demon wheeling round in my skull as well. It's only my friends who are lucky.

MOLLY: But don't you think two lovers, say, can stay beautiful to each other?

O'RIORDON: For a while, maybe, but they can't stay blind for ever.

MOLLY: Michael, you're a bitter cynic. Away with you.

O'RIORDON: Ah, many's the lying lover saying this moment into someone's believing ear: 'You'll always be beautiful to me, my darling, as you are this moment,' and up she climbs on the high wall of hope. O, Humpty-Dumpty!

MOLLY: When will the two halves of you meet? Cynical

advice with one hand and perpetual youth with the other. Be consistent, now.

O'RIORDON: I never let my right hand know what my left hand's giving.

MOLLY: All the same, *I* shall not be deterred from falling in love –

O'RIORDON: I hope you won't.

MOLLY: Not even by my only big brother!

O'RIORDON: In the name of God, I'm not your brother and never have been!

MOLLY: Never?

O'RIORDON: Well, I may have been once, but not now.

MOLLY: So, so, you're drifting away from me.
    [*She hears* JOHNNY *approaching and runs to the door, so does not hear* O'RIORDON'S *next words.*]

O'RIORDON: Not away, Molly – towards. I –

MOLLY: Oh, here's Johnny at last. Hello, you.
    [*Enter* JOHNNY.]

JOHNNY: Hello, you. Hello, Michael. It's a rare spring day out. You should have come with us.

O'RIORDON: Have you gone soft-hearted towards the rabbit population, that you try to shoot them from horseback?

JOHNNY: We just thought it'd be more fun.

O'RIORDON: Try bow-and-arrow next time, and we'll not have rabbit pie ever again.

JOHNNY: Not a bad idea, that. It's my top-unfavourite pie.

O'RIORDON: Top-unfavourite? God help us, and you say we talk backwards.

JOHNNY: Any tea on the hob?

MOLLY: I'll make some fresh: your pampered palate won't like this.

JOHNNY: No, no, please. I'm beginning to like Shamus's stew.

MOLLY: But we have a reputation for hospitality in this country, even towards our friends.
    [*Exit* MOLLY.]

JOHNNY: Well, Michael, I never thought prison life could be so pleasant.

O'RIORDON: I don't think it is as a rule. They weren't nearly so hospitable to me back in '16. Still, if we're not kind to our enemies, how shall we ever be kind to our friends, tell me that.

JOHNNY: How, indeed? You know, it's absurd to say so, but these three months have been the happiest of my life, thanks to you and Molly. I lie in bed and bless that surly-looking lad who stuck a cold gun-barrel in the back of my neck on a winter night three months ago. A surly angel, he was, opening the gate of an unexpected Paradise. He led me into prison and freedom.

O'RIORDON: We're all in prison together, Johnny, one way or the other. I'm a prisoner of the dark, and we're all prisoners of the body, are we not? And if we escape into the mind we find ourselves inside some thick-walled philosophy. And if we escape from life itself, there we are behind the tall bars of eternity. It's a terrible incarcerated existence! Still, so long as we can sing in our cages we shall be happy enough, I daresay, so why worry.

JOHNNY: I don't worry, Michael, except by fits and starts. That clash with the Tans a week back worried me a bit. It seemed so unreal – or was it my happiness here that had been unreal? Anyway, the two worlds seemed so very different and the clash as disastrous as two planets colliding. Now here we are back on our course again. Will there be another collision?

O'RIORDON: You know well enough, Johnny, I can't discuss military secrets with you. Though why the hell not, I don't know. If it came to a fight here in these grounds, which side would you be on? Not with the Tans, I'll be bound.

JOHNNY: No, not with them.

O'RIORDON: No. Still, you're officially what Scanlon calls a khaki cut-throat.

F

JOHNNY: Who's Scanlon, for God's sake?

O'RIORDON: Sean Kelly's aide. They arrived last night. You'll never persuade him to like you. 'Can any good,' says he, 'come out of England?'

JOHNNY: That's a boomerang insult. Isn't that what the Pharisees said – 'Can any good come out of Galilee?'

O'RIORDON: It may be. But then you Protestant fellers always know your Bible so much better than we do.

JOHNNY: You may tell me nothing, Michael, but Sean Kelly's not come here for the holiday. I know how important he is from the size of the reward offered – even more, I may say, than they offer for you.

O'RIORDON: If it's any sop to your curiosity, Johnny, I know at the moment as little as you do: I'm not on the active list and why should I know any more than I have to? One mouth less to give away the Cause.

[*Enter* MOLLY *with tea.*]

MOLLY: Tea, made in the best English manner, according to Mrs Beeton.

JOHNNY: Thanks, but don't keep reminding me I'm a foreigner. I don't like the feel of it.

MOLLY: You'll be singing 'Wrap the Green Flag Round Me, Boys', before you leave here. I can see it coming. Johnny O'Tregarthen, the English Emigrant.

O'RIORDON: There's a song in that.

MOLLY: There's a song in everything this morning. Look at all the blossom in the garden; [*switching with natural tact to* O'RIORDON's *range of sense*] you can smell the lilac from here. And there's not a bird has kept his throat quiet – listen. It has a lovely feeling of life beginning, as if this were the first morning that ever was.

O'RIORDON: Maybe it is. Maybe God created the world five minutes ago, complete with memories and records and fossils. That's a fine theory – disprove me that one.

JOHNNY: I don't want to, Michael. This feels so like the

first morning I'm willing to believe it is. Let's not argue, let's just enjoy. This tea is as good as my mother made.

MOLLY: You forget the world began five minutes ago: this is the first cup ever; the pristine, original, first pot of tea ever brewed, according to God's instructions in Mrs Beeton.

O'RIORDON: In that case, I must have a taste. This is something not to be missed.

MOLLY: We must all drink. Here's a toast to creation – may it prove a happy idea. [*They drink.*]

O'RIORDON: As tingling and delicious on the palate as ever was the first draught of water to Adam himself by the crystal springs of Eden!

MOLLY: As soft and comforting as the Grace of God to an old one dying after seventy years of mortal sin!

JOHNNY: Good tea!

MOLLY: Oh, the sun's gone in. What a thick cloud suddenly – nearly as bad as the English climate.

JOHNNY: Jolly nearly.

MOLLY: A storm coming up, maybe.

O'RIORDON: Perhaps God's tired of the world already, and is going to end it ten minutes precisely from now. [*The clock strikes eleven.*]

MOLLY: Oh, Michael, don't. That clock terrified me. Eleven o'clock, too – the eleventh hour.

JOHNNY: You know, it feels like evening: that cloud's made it twilight.

O'RIORDON: Then, let's treat it like evening. It's all one to me. Let's gather the shadows around us and be comfortable.

JOHNNY [*to* MOLLY]: Here, share my shadow. [*She sits beside him.*] Now, Michael, as it's cosy evening-time, how about a song?

MOLLY: Yes, come on, Michael. Where's your harp?

O'RIORDON: I left her by the window, twangling softly to every breeze that blows. Here she is, my girleen. A sad song or a merry one?

MOLLY: Oh, a sad one, of course, a sad one.

JOHNNY: Yes, let's have a sad one, the sadder the better.

[O'RIORDON *twangs a few notes of ' The Salley Gardens'*.]

O'RIORDON [*sings*]:

Down by the salley gardens my love and I did meet,
She passed the salley gardens with little snow-white feet,
She bid me take love easy, as the leaves grow on the tree,
But I, being young and foolish, with her would not agree.
In a field by the river, my love and I did stand,
And on my leaning shoulder she laid her snow-white hand,
She bid me take life easy, as the grass grows on the weirs,
But I was young and foolish, and now am full of tears.*

[*During the first verse* JOHNNY *and* MOLLY *hold hands.
During the second, a big man appears in the shadows on the
stairs, indistinct, watching.*]

KELLY [*as the song finishes*]:

For the great Gaels of Ireland
Are the men that God made mad,
For all their wars are merry
And all their songs are sad.†

O'RIORDON: Sean! Ah, what are you doing, creeping up on
us like Nemesis himself. As if we hadn't enough to worry
us, and the end of the world on us and all.

KELLY: What, again? Is that why you're singing? To keep
your spirits up on the deck of a sinking world?

O'RIORDON: Since when did anyone need a reason for singing? And I'm not stopping just because the Lord has thrown
a hood over my cage. This is my cousin – where are you,
girl?

MOLLY: Here.

O'RIORDON: Molly Kinsella, and Captain John Tregarthen –
Sean Kelly.

KELLY [*to* MOLLY]: Hello. [*To* JOHNNY]: Captain Tregarthen?

* 'The Salley Gardens': words by W. B. Yeats.
† From 'Ballad of the White Horse' by G. K. Chesterton.

JOHNNY: Of the British Army.

KELLY: So, so, I'd forgotten you were here. [*Satirically*]: Any complaints about your treatment?

JOHNNY: None at all.

KELLY [*looking from* MOLLY *to* JOHNNY *and back again*]: None.

O'RIORDON: Well, Sean, where have you been all the morning?

KELLY: Oh, spying the land, spying the land. And I've just been over this palace. In the name of God, what are you doing with eight lavatories?

O'RIORDON: Oh, didn't you know? Tolly owns this house. *The* Tolly, whose name is writ in porcelain from here to China.

KELLY: But why, if I may ask, are all eight in different colours?

O'RIORDON: They remind him of home: each one of the family has his very own.

KELLY: Well, I hope for Old Ireland's sake, we'll avoid the green one.

MOLLY: We'll leave you, Mr Kelly. I'm sure you've more important things on your mind.

KELLY: There are times when there's nothing more important, but this isn't one of them.

MOLLY: We'll come back later, then. See you at lunch, maybe.

O'RIORDON: Good-bye for the time. Good-bye, Johnny.

JOHNNY: *Au revoir.*

[*Exeunt* MOLLY *and* JOHNNY.]

O'RIORDON: Well, Sean, what brings you this far north?

KELLY: Captain Tregarthen seems to be making himself at home.

O'RIORDON: That's what I want. He's a grand lad.

KELLY: Your cousin looks blooming.

O'RIORDON [*sad*]: Yes, I'm sure.

KELLY: Tell me, did you ever follow up what you told me about her a while back?

O'RIORDON: That was before – There was so much fighting to do that I put off asking her, and how the hell can I
ask her for a wife now?

KELLY: Why not?

O'RIORDON: Oh, once or twice I've tried. Then the moment
slips away. You see, Sean, I've been so long a kind of an elder
brother that I don't think she'll know me another way. Or
maybe she will – I don't know. Only this morning, the talk
seemed to turn the right way, but just as I'd screwed up my
nerve, in came Johnny.

KELLY: In came Johnny.

O'RIORDON: And now my nerves have gone slack again!

KELLY: Michael, would you like me to have him transferred?

O'RIORDON: Who?

KELLY: Captain Tregarthen.

O'RIORDON: Dear Lord, no. He's a friend of mine. I wouldn't
lose him for the world. What a queer thing to say suddenly. Why should I want to lose him?

KELLY: Oh, no reason. It's unwise to be too fond of an
enemy, that's all. But it seems to me, Michael, if I may bend
the subject backward to yourself, that your heart still points
the same way it did when last you talked to me, so I should
lose no time, but follow it.

O'RIORDON: Ah, sure, I know that well enough. But how
can I be sure she wouldn't say 'Yes' out of pity? I couldn't
bear not to be able to see her eyes when I asked. How am I
to guess at the surprise and distress that might come first to
her face, to be driven out maybe by a comfortable pity that
isn't love.

KELLY: Now, this isn't like you, Michael. You ought to be
the same sort of a lover as you were a fighter. By God, I
envied you that splendid kind of a madness that came on
you when you fought: immemorial ancestors rode shouting along your veins, and came hosting to the heart. That's
the way a man ought to fight. And there was me beside

you, as excited as if I was doing mental arithmetic – 'forsooth, a great arithmetician', adding a wound here, subtracting a life there, applying the square root of pain to the result of dividing a man from his own. And at the end of the battle, I could tell you the answer to the third point of decimation. There'd be some excuse for me acting as you are, in the way of love: I'm a cold one, and I've spent my life trying to make myself feel sorrow and love and the rest, and stifling in the attempt.

O'RIORDON: I could love once as I fought, maybe; but the heart is a child and I suppose the dark makes it afraid. Anyway, what are you trying to make yourself? As cold a trout as ever glittered in silver suffocation on a grass-green world? Cold hearts don't fight for lost causes as you've done, do they now: Sean Kelly, soldier of fortune, lost causes only considered!

KELLY: Just hoping I could make myself feel, Michael, that's all. And I can't: every cause I fight for wins – it's terrible!

O'RIORDON: And what about the present one? I take it you came up in your official capacity as an arithmetician?

KELLY: I did, indeed. But your own problem looms larger in my mind at the moment.

O'RIORDON: Sure, that's a false perspective, Sean. When you're lying on the grass, a flower an inch or two from your eye can blot out a mountain a mile or two away. So let's just pluck my tiny problem, shall we, and look at the mountain?

KELLY: Pluck your problem? Well, I wish I could. However, to business. We have information about the activities of the Tans in this area. The force that visited here a week ago was only a reconnaissance. They are to be reinforced by a detachment that landed last night at Gallyn Bay. They have joined and are coming overland. An hour ago they had reached Dalgenny. Their object is to clean up this headquarters.

O'RIORDON: So! Poor Tolly!

KELLY: We'll be outnumbered, of course, so the best chance is an ambush. I've gathered all available men and they're waiting armed in the wood to the east of the house. We've plenty of time. The problem is simply to choose our point of ambush. Now, you know this countryside like your own body, so I want your advice. I went very quickly over the land last night. I had thought of Clon Wood as the road curves through it. What do you think?

O'RIORDON: There's too much cover for them as well as us, once we open fire.

KELLY: Where, then?

O'RIORDON: What about Glasfont Bridge, which they must cross?

KELLY: Isn't that dangerously close to here?

O'RIORDON: That may lure them into thinking we're unprepared.

KELLY: True, it may.

O'RIORDON: And it's by far the best point of ambush. You can put half your men this side of the bridge, half the other, in the wood to the left of the road. Allow the Tans to cross, open fire from this side, and as they retreat back over the bridge open up from the other side. It should be a double surprise.

KELLY: Surprise – what a darling understatement! Yes, we'll lift their eyebrows for them! I remember the spot well. Where is it on the map now? Oh yes. Well, that gives us plenty of time. The Tans can't be further than Glaslough by now, and we get hourly reports. If we are in position by three this afternoon, that will be ample time. [*Calls off*]: Scanlon!

SCANLON [*off*]: Coming, sir.

   [*Enter* SCANLON, *lean, dark, shy, devoted to Kelly, slightly hysterical fanatic.*]

KELLY: Stand by until after lunch. Reassemble at two o'clock.

We ambush at Glasfont Bridge. But tell no one as yet – tongues are too long.

SCANLON: Ah, thank God, that'll give time for the priest to hear confessions. We were afraid we'd have to go too soon, with only a general absolution, maybe.

[*Exit.*]

KELLY: Dear Scanlon! He takes his faith neat – it's too much for a weak head.

O'RIORDON: Are you going yourself?

KELLY: To confession? I don't think so. I don't see why I should break a custom. It's ten years now since I went.

O'RIORDON: Customs are made to be broken.

KELLY: Not by me. Though I nearly broke it in '16, after the cold-faced Colonel at the Court Martial said 'That you be taken from this place and shot'. But the reprieve came and the crisis passed.

O'RIORDON: Well, God give you a fine comfy death-bed!

KELLY: Not that I don't believe it all – I do, of course. But to confess at all, you've got to be sorry for your sins, and I've never in my life been sorry for anything.

O'RIORDON: One of those emotions you pretend you don't feel?

KELLY: But I don't. You mustn't paint your friends as you want them to be, Michael. See them as they are, then love them if you can. Quite honestly, I've never been sorry for anything. Sorrow and remorse, the soft sisters, seem quite dead in me – or maybe they were never born.

O'RIORDON: More likely just asleep. That's it, Sean, they're sleeping beauties, awaiting the kiss of the prince! How's that?

KELLY: Pretty, but a bloody lie, I fear. No, I wish to God I *could* just once weep to turn the world anti-clockwise and undo something I'd done. Sometimes I'm tempted to do something terrible, just in the hope. Maybe I will, some day – maybe I will.

[*Enter* SCANLON, *running.*]

What is it, for God's sake, that you fling yourself in here without orders?

SCANLON: Sorry, sir, but dispatches with terrible news – O God, terrible news.

KELLY: Calm your hysterics and say what you've got to say.

SCANLON: It's Keogh, M'Gill and O'Shea, sir. The bastards have shot them in cold blood. The news has come up like a fire from Dublin.

[KELLY *snatches documents.*]

O'RIORDON: Keogh, M'Gill and O'Shea! Dear God, they can't be – they can't! Were they captured, or what?

SCANLON: Captured and shot in cold blood. Riddled with bullets and not allowed to see the priest. It's the blackest crime –

O'RIORDON: But prisoners of war! They've never shot prisoners of war!

SCANLON: It's the Tans. It's the Tans, God damn them to hell.

O'RIORDON: God rest their souls – M'Gill –

KELLY [*violently*]: Christ, can't I even feel grief when three of my best friends are shot? Well, Michael, you're all I've left now of the great days, you and Kevin Byrne – all I've left. And what's this? [*Reads on.*] 'To repay death with death, a life for a life, three British Army officers or N.C.O's to be chosen by lottery.'

O'RIORDON: What's that?

KELLY: Reprisals. Stupid.

SCANLON: Stupid, sir? It's God's justice, that's what it is.

O'RIORDON: Shut up, will you? Sean, what is it? What's going to happen?

KELLY: Hysterics at Headquarters. The stupidity of anger. Oh, now I see why they've written at such length to me about it. They think I'll have no compunction, and they're right, I suppose. They've deputed me to carry out the death lottery, assisted by the two senior officers on the spot, and that, gentlemen, means you.

O'RIORDON: Us! But, Sean, we –

KELLY: There can be no argument. These are clear orders. Stupid or not, they must be carried out. We are sworn to do that.

SCANLON: Thanks be to God, I'll have a hand in the revenging of my comrades.

O'RIORDON: In the name of Christ, shut up your exulting.

KELLY: 'Executions' – listen, gentlemen – 'to be carried out within three days, by whatever officer is in charge of the condemned men.' Ah! they've thoughtfully enclosed a list of officers and N.C.O. prisoners. Not, I see, in alphabetical order; shuffled anyhow, Colonel lying by Corporal like a king by a six in a pack of cards. Well, gentlemen, we've time before lunch; shall we proceed forthwith? Sit down. Now, I suggest one of us takes a pin and pricks the dead. To be sure we're impartial, will you oblige, Michael?

O'RIORDON: Sean, in God's name let's question these orders. We can't shoot British Army men for what the Tans have done.

KELLY: I recognize no difference.

O'RIORDON: Headquarters will repent at leisure – they're bound to.

KELLY: You know the General, and you know he won't. What's the worry? A flight of grey bullets that nest in the heart is as good a way to die as any – if there be good ways to die. In any case, public anger will demand a sacrifice, so let's bow to the wind. And before we start, let's get one point clear. Whoever the pin finds must be the ones who die. There must be no shuffling and no exceptions. We must simply be what the General so eloquently but so inaccurately calls 'the instruments of God's justice'. Are we ready? It's no use, Michael, we're bound by oath to our orders, therefore the responsibility is not ours. Remember, we are bound by oath. Go ahead – we're waiting. [O'RIORDON *pricks one*.] Scanlon, take down the names as I call them. Major Peter Beardmore.

SCANLON: Major? Is that all right? – Major? –

KELLY: Field rank is no passport to immortality. Write him down.

SCANLON [*writing*]: Major Peter Beardmore.

KELLY: Next. [O'RIORDON *pricks another*.] Not near anyone. Again. [O'RIORDON *pricks again*.] Sergeant Neville de Courcy. A fine name for a Sergeant. Changed it by Deed Poll, maybe. However, he'll soon join the aristocracy of the Saints.

SCANLON [*writing*]: Sergeant Neville de Courcy.

O'RIORDON: Sean, for pity's sake –

KELLY: No, Michael, if I had pity to give I still could not give it. Whoever I'm on oath to serve, I serve, and so must you. Next.

[*Enter* TOLLY *and* SHAMUS *with the bags.*]

TOLLY: Get the bags on to the landing. I'll just have to go to-morrow, that's all. Don't let me interrupt you, gentlemen, I only own this house.

KELLY [*softly*]: Next.

SHAMUS: I'm sorry, sorr, but how was I to know Tim would climb without warning on the water wagon?

[*Exeunt* TOLLY *and* SHAMUS *upstairs.*]

KELLY: Next.

[O'RIORDON *pricks another.*]

KELLY [*looks at the paper, then looks for a long moment fixedly at* O'RIORDON; *turns abruptly to* SCANLON]: Captain John Tregarthen.

O'RIORDON [*cries*]: Oh, no –

[*Enter* JOHNNY *and* MOLLY *excitedly, hand in hand.*]

MOLLY [*as she enters*]: Michael, Michael, are you there? We've news for you.

JOHNNY: Great news.

MOLLY: Ah, sorry. We'll tell you after. God bless you, Michael, darling. Poor Tolly has missed his train. [*They laugh together and go out.*]

SCANLON: Captain John – ?

KELLY: Tregarthen.

SCANLON [*writing*]: Treg-arth-en. [*As* O'RIORDON *stands
rigid and* SCANLON *ignorantly writes*

THE CURTAIN FALLS

ACT TWO

Same scene, afternoon of the same day.

> [SHAMUS *is polishing silver in his green baize apron.*]
> [*Enter* MOLLY *from the garden.*]

MOLLY: Oh, Shamus, have you seen Mr Michael anywhere?

SHAMUS: Mr Michael? Now, let me see. I last saw him – when was it? Just before Mr Tolly left for the station, it was. They was talking here and meself was harnessing the trap.

MOLLY: Not since then? That's no use.

SHAMUS: Wait, now. Didn't I see him as I came back – with Kelly himself and another lad, in this very room?

MOLLY: Well, *we* saw him then, but no sign since. He's had no lunch.

SHAMUS: Ah, now, that won't do. A man should never miss the ritual of a good meal.

JOHNNY [*coming downstairs*]: No sign upstairs. But I still don't know my way around this labyrinth. I may have missed a whole wing.

MOLLY: Well, we can tell him later, love. He must be upset about something – bad news, maybe, of some friend of his fighting.

JOHNNY: Yes. The air seemed a bit tense when we came in, I thought. Never mind. Sweet news can wait, like good wine.

SHAMUS: And did you have some of that port I decanted to-day?

MOLLY: We did indeed. We were celebrating.

SHAMUS: It had a grand colour to it. Y'know, when I was in prison, after holding a gun for Ireland in '16, I used to sit and look through me bars at the green hills and the red sunsets and the silver stars. And I'd think of me baize apron, and decanting me port, and polishing me spoons. Then I'd lie in me narrow bed at night, and dream of tying the green hills around me waist, and decanting the sunset itself, and polishing the millions of the firmament. Ah, it was a grand ceremonious dream! And a terrible waking-up!

MOLLY [*to* JOHNNY]: Here, hold a star in your hand. [*Gives him a spoon.*]

JOHNNY: And one for you. May they never go out.

MOLLY: Let's keep these two spoons, shall we? – for luck. We'll keep them, Shamus.

SHAMUS: You can, of course, Miss Molly. Sure they don't belong to me. And may they bring you great luck. I'll leave the rest to glitter on the table and comfort the room. 'Tis still a black day outside. And rumour's in the air, too, about the Tans coming. Do you not hear how quiet it is? The soldiers is about their business, with Kelly himself at their head.

JOHNNY: Then we'd better keep within doors.

MOLLY: Nothing's going to stop me looking out of the window, if I hear things stirring.

JOHNNY: No, I think we should all be confined to barracks – at least until they come back. I wish Michael were in.

SHAMUS: I'll keep in the house, sorr. And Mr Tolly'll be close in, too, never fear. If I see Mr Michael, will I say you're looking for him?

MOLLY: Please. God bless you.

SHAMUS: And God bless *you*.

[*Exit* SHAMUS.]

MOLLY: Darling Shamus, with his hands full of stars.

JOHNNY: He's a great romancer. Michael thinks he was in gaol for looting.

MOLLY: Ah, what matter? It would have been a fine ritual, looting! And he's a great little soul.

JOHNNY [*holding up his spoon*]: Isn't this the sign for a wedding?

MOLLY [*softly*]: Yes – please.
   [*They kiss.*]

JOHNNY: Oh, Molly, darling, I wish we were away, back in England. I want to love you in peace.

MOLLY: Ah, sure, don't worry about a little brush with the Tans. I can't say I like Sean Kelly, but I'd trust him to guard me. Anyway, look, we have our own little private sky full of stars that no cloud can cover and no storm disturb, set there and charted by Astronomer Shamus himself. See, there's Orion with his belt and sword.

JOHNNY: And there's the Plough turned upside down.

MOLLY: Oh dear, that means rain! And look, a whole Pleiades of Apostle spoons.

JOHNNY: And here's a star that's not in the common sky at all. A new planet swims into our ken. What shall we call it?

MOLLY: Grace Before Meals.

JOHNNY: Why on earth?

MOLLY: It's a soup spoon.

JOHNNY: Good enough. What a gift Michael has. He was right when he said the world began to-day. For us it did. Everything looks somehow strange and pristine – see? The light in this room is like no light I've ever seen: a sort of violet, from the storm-cloud outside and the light inside.

MOLLY: Our love against the thunder! We'll take up the challenge! Tell me now, where are we going to live in England? Can the gentleman in khaki give me the luxury to which I've been accustomed?

JOHNNY: Oh, a very different sort of luxury – as different as England from Ireland. First of all, just as soon as I get out of here I shall resign my commission. I'd had enough of soldiering in my first week.

MOLLY: Poor darling, why did you go on?

JOHNNY: Oh, just inertia. The younger son of a wealthy farmer, no inheritance – you know. And I badly wanted to stay on the farm.

MOLLY: Well, go on, tell me where we're going to live. I want to ogle the future.

JOHNNY: It'll be the farm, darling. My elder brother was killed in '18, and my father is moving towards seventy now and dearly wants me home. So the farm it'll be. You'll love my father: he has the fiercest nose and moustache that you ever saw, but the softest eyes.

MOLLY: Oh, I love him already.

JOHNNY: The farm's on a hill in Buckinghamshire. On a clear day you can see London, and with the help of a telescope my father has in his bedroom you can even see St Paul's.

MOLLY: A telescope in his bedroom?

JOHNNY: Yes. He watches the stars, too. He'd never admit it, but he'd use it to watch for us when we came home on leave.

MOLLY: The darling. So, I shall be able to drive into London and buy up the town. I hope you have a coach and four.

JOHNNY: My darling, we have a Rolls-Royce, a great thing big enough to carry a coffin.

MOLLY: God love us. A motor-propelled vehicle. That's an adventure I've never had.

JOHNNY: It'll be one of many, love. And the village of Broome, near my home, has the loveliest old church with a square tower, and there's a great coloured sun-dial on its side with 'The Night Cometh' underneath. Why are sun-dials always so gloomy?

MOLLY: Sure, we don't need an old sun-dial to tell us that. Anyway, the day looks more glorious because of it. [*Softly*]: Dearest Johnny! Is the old church with the tower where you're thinking of marrying me?

JOHNNY: No, don't worry, There's a Catholic Chapel on the edge of the village, made of corrugated iron. That'll be our Cathedral. Satisfied?

MOLLY: Sounds like Heaven itself. And we'll try to make it so, shall we?

G

JOHNNY: We will. Just as soon as these troubles are over –
and they can't last much longer – we'll sail. What a pity
we can't take Michael with us. I shall miss him.

MOLLY: He can come and be Godfather to our first.

JOHNNY [*laughing*]: Yes. My word, I didn't know when I
used to hear his name so often that I'd meet him like this.
His name and Kelly's are legends among the British fighting here. Did you know? And I felt almost ashamed when
amateur soldiers were legendary heroes, and I, whose
business was supposed to be soldiering, looked on fighting
with dread. You won't stop loving me, will you, if I confess how glad I was to be taken prisoner?

MOLLY: There's nothing in God's world could stop me loving
you. And I hope you *are* glad. Sure, how else could we have
met?

JOHNNY: I suffered nightmares for those I was shooting at.
I never got used to it. And nightmares, too, for myself
being shot at. I often dreamed of a great blue eye looking
through gunsights at my own heart.

MOLLY: Never mind, love, it's all over now.

JOHNNY: Yes, all over.

   [*Thunder. Two rolls.*]

MOLLY: Forget the storm outside. Only remember the stars
in the room. [*A gesture to the spoons.*] They represent our
future and they are bright and fixed. Cheer up, now.

JOHNNY: Sorry, darling. I'm just annoyed with myself that
suddenly I'm not standing tiptoe on the world's top. I
should be. I have the loveliest girl that ever shot rabbits
from horseback to love me –

MOLLY: Johnny! That doesn't leave a deal of competition.

JOHNNY: But the thunder outside seems to have settled in
here [*Touches his heart.*] Why? Riddle me that one, as
Michael would say.

MOLLY: A deep depression is approaching Heartland. Really,
darling, you call us superstitious, but there's not a people on

earth to touch the English. You can't see a cloud without thinking of the black-plumed horses, or a silver bough of lightning itself without seeing a raven perched there.

JOHNNY: Now, that's not true. And to prove it, I shall snap at once out of my small depression by the one sure way. [*He kisses her.*]

MOLLY: Still depressed?

JOHNNY: Of course, if that's the remedy. [*They laugh.*]

MOLLY: That's better.

JOHNNY: Darling, why can't we be married here – soon?

MOLLY: Ah, sure, you don't know how hard it is in Ireland. A mixed marriage is tough to get a dispensation for when times are good – and times, as you may have heard, are not good. No, let's enjoy our engagement, shall we? Sure, every time of life has its own magic. This is the magic of betrothal. In England, surely, we'll get a dispensation for the asking.

JOHNNY: I hope you're right. I've never asked for one before.

MOLLY: It will not be long, love, till our wedding day. Remember the song? We'll wait for our little Cathedral of corrugated iron in Broome village; and your Da and Michael, too, I hope can be there. And the Chapel will be warm with our joy long after we've driven off in our Rolls-Royce for the honeymoon.

JOHNNY: And where will that be?

MOLLY: In Heaven, of course. Where else?

JOHNNY: No, seriously, where would you like?

MOLLY: Ah, sure, I couldn't dream of deciding yet. I'll dream of Venice and Capri and Paris and Morocco. I shall dream! [*There is a clap of thunder.*]

JOHNNY: Here it comes. We'd better light the lamp. [*Does so.*] Twilight after lunch. There's someone in the drive. [*Goes to the window.*] It's Michael, at last, thank Heaven. Oh, Tolly has buttonholed him.

MOLLY: Poor Michael. Let's stand in the alcove and surprise them.

TOLLY [*entering*]: For Heaven's sake, let's get inside. There'll be a downpour. Some angel will pull the chain at any moment. [*Pause.*] Oh dear, who said the Irish had a sense of humour? [O'RIORDON *enters.*] Now that we have a moment free from the problems of your little war, I want to talk about important things. What are we going to do about the little beech wood across the lawn?

O'RIORDON: Do about it?

TOLLY: Yes. Timber fetches a lot these days, and it's doing nothing to earn its keep. I suggest we have it down.

O'RIORDON: For God's sake, let it live. There's enough murder being done without yourself starting it.

TOLLY: Really, O'Riordon! It's becoming increasingly difficult to talk sense with you at all. Give me one good reason why it shouldn't be cut down.

O'RIORDON: It's beautiful, that's good enough. Do you *need* the money?

TOLLY: I don't *need* it —

O'RIORDON: Well, then!

TOLLY: It's a mystery to me how you run this place so well. Still, you live here more than I do, so I'll reprieve the beech wood. How's that?

O'RIORDON: Thanks.

TOLLY: And there's the other matter —

O'RIORDON: Not now, for God's sake, not now. I'm sorry — I'm not myself, but not now, please!

TOLLY: Oh, very well, of course. [*Pause.*]

O'RIORDON: What is there so warm in this room?

TOLLY: Someone's lit the lamp.

O'RIORDON: Oh, is it that dark? That should help Kelly.

MOLLY [*from the alcove*]: Michael.

O'RIORDON: Molly! Sure, I thought — more than the lamp was warming the room.

MOLLY: And more than me! Johnny, tell them!

O'RIORDON: Johnny –

JOHNNY: No, *you*!

MOLLY: Well, I'll not wait to argue. Michael, darling, and Mr Tolly, pray silence for good news. Johnny and I are engaged. [*Silence.*] To be married. Are you dumb, or what?

TOLLY: Well, well. Well I never. Well, I never did. That's fine. My congratulations. I hope that means England and Ireland will get on better in future. [*To* JOHNNY]: We've not met before, have we? I'm glad it should be on so pleasant an occasion.

MOLLY: Well, Michael, haven't you a word to say?

O'RIORDON: Yes, yes –

JOHNNY: The news has floored him. Now, Michael, don't tell me you didn't guess.

O'RIORDON: Sure, I'm sorry, Johnny. I – I'm not well, that's all.

MOLLY: Michael – !

O'RIORDON: Bad news of some dear friends dead, and others in great danger. I'm glad, of course. God bless you.

MOLLY: We're sorry for your trouble, Michael, and wish we could share it.

O'RIORDON: Please, could I speak to you, Johnny?

JOHNNY: Go ahead.

O'RIORDON: No, just to you, Johnny. Tolly, will you see Molly safe? There'll be shooting nearby soon. Please.

TOLLY: Oh dear, will there? Of course. Will you trust me with your fiancée, Captain?

JOHNNY: Yes, and I trust *her* with *you*.

MOLLY: See you soon, love. We'll wait in the Round Room. 'Bye, Michael darling.

[*Exeunt* MOLLY *and* TOLLY.]

O'RIORDON: Are they well gone?

JOHNNY: Yes. What is it, Michael? Can I help?

O'RIORDON: Oh, dear Christ –

JOHNNY: What is it, Michael? Tell me.

O'RIORDON: I've trod the grass bare trying to think my way out of this. Johnny, listen. After what you've told me about you and Molly, there's one way only – one way only – and you must promise me to take it. Johnny, promise me.

JOHNNY: Out of what? I'll do anything in the world for you. Just say the word.

O'RIORDON: You must leave here now – now this minute – and run for the border. Take the fastest horse – Maeve is fresh – and ride west to Ballygenny, then north to Belfast –

JOHNNY: But, Michael – why –

O'RIORDON: Johnny, in the name of God, don't question me, but go. The horse you can leave in any stable, there, and just let me know by the post where she is. I'll get her back.

JOHNNY: Michael, wait. You're not talking sense. You can't expect me to run off on a chase like this without telling me more. Why am I going? When do I come back? Is it some job only I can do? Is it to do with the war? Or what?

O'RIORDON: Look now, do you trust me?

JOHNNY: Of course.

O'RIORDON: Then you will go at once and ask no questions. What's the time now: tell me.

JOHNNY: Three o'clock. If that old clock's right.

O'RIORDON: At once, then – at once. O God, why couldn't I have told you before? What in God's world does an oath of honour weigh against a friend's life? I don't know, I don't know at all. I've lost my way surely.

JOHNNY: A friend's life? Michael, what do you mean?

O'RIORDON: You said you trusted me –

JOHNNY: I do.

O'RIORDON: Then saddle the horse and go. Stay in Belfast.

Or better, in England, till all these troubles are over and done.

JOHNNY: I'm sorry, Michael, you're not yourself. I must know more. Apart from anything else, I've given my parole – you know I can't break that.

O'RIORDON: Your parole! Sure I don't give a thraneen for it – and nor must you, not now!

JOHNNY: But I must, Michael. I've been brought up to believe in it, and nothing I know will make me break mine.

O'RIORDON: Listen, do you want Molly to be happy?

JOHNNY: You know the answer to that.

O'RIORDON: Then believe me, Johnny, if you're not to break her heart for ever you'll do as I say.

JOHNNY: Michael, I don't stir a foot from here until you tell me what this means.

O'RIORDON: You're wasting time, Johnny – precious time –

JOHNNY: Not a foot, Michael, till you tell me what it means. [Pause.]

O'RIORDON: It means your life's in jeopardy. It means that if you don't run now you'll be dead in three days. It means that the blind hates of war have trapped us both: that I must break my oath to the Army and you must break your parole to me, to save three hearts being broken for ever. That's what it means. In the name of God, don't you see now why you must ride for the Border as fast as Maeve can take you?

JOHNNY: But I'm a prisoner of war. How can I be in danger?

O'RIORDON: Reprisals, Johnny, just reprisals. The ugliest word in the whole ugly jargon of war. Three Irish officers were shot by the Tans, so three British prisoners were chosen by lottery to follow them.

JOHNNY: And you mean my name – ?

O'RIORDON: Yes. Your name, O, God, why can't men just love each other? A man can walk further from Christ with

one prick of a pin in malice than a lifetime of the sins of love will take him. So now, Johnny, dear, will you go, and go with my love and Molly's to speed you?
[*Thunder.*]

JOHNNY: I – I can't run, Michael. They surely won't carry it through.

O'RIORDON: Kelly will. I've known him many years, and I know Kelly will. That's why you must go before the fighting starts. Don't you see? For he'll be back, as sure as the night comes. It'll take more than the bullet of a Tan to finish Sean Kelly.

JOHNNY: No, Michael, I can't run. I must fight it. I'll see Kelly when he comes back. There must be a way –

O'RIORDON: Johnny, you fool, you fool.

JOHNNY: And if I run, won't they prick another's name? [*Silence.*] Won't they? [*Silence.*] No, I can't run.
[*Thunder. Shots begin – a strong fusillade.*]

O'RIORDON: Christ alive, it's started! 'Tis too late now. O, why didn't I tell you at once? We've lost the best chance there was. We've lost it –

JOHNNY: It would have made no difference, Michael. Don't blame yourself, it would have made no difference.

O'RIORDON: We'll find a way, Johnny – we'll find a way. If it's the last thing I do, I'll see this doesn't happen. You're still in my charge, remember – we'll find a way. Now go and see Molly safe, will you? Glasfont Bridge, where they're ambushing, is less than a bullet's throw from here.

JOHNNY: Will you come with me?

O'RIORDON: No, I'll stay here. I'd rather stay alone. Go, Johnny, and may God help us to find our way out of this darkness.
[JOHNNY *goes. A second strong fusillade.* O'RIORDON *goes to the window, listens. As the shots continue, he sits by his harp and plays – stops again to listen, and continues playing – stops again as he hears steps outside.*]

1ST TAN [*off*]: It's a bastard ambush. Quick, inside.
  [*The two enter. The first, a small, vicious sadist; the second, a thug.*]

2ND TAN: Where is it, eh?

1ST TAN: The bridge. The one advantage of being a scout, boy: when the main body's ambushed, you're somewhere else. Up to the landing window, and I'll take this one. [*Sees* O'RIORDON.] Well, God send us a fine day, who have we here? And all unarmed, except for his little harp.

2ND TAN: Who is it, eh?

1ST TAN: Now, don't tell me you don't recognize that face! Haven't you seen it on the posters? Reward – dead or alive – Keep your gun trained on him, boy, he's one of the Tigers.

2ND TAN: No, who is he? Posters all look alike to me.

1ST TAN: The great Michael O'Riordon, all alone, guarding H.Q. with a loaded harp.

2ND TAN: O'Riordon? You don't mean – ?

1ST TAN: I do mean. And what are you doing, Mr O'Riordon sir, all out of the battle? Have you a little headache? [*Silence. Throughout this scene* O'RIORDON *sits still as a loaded field-gun.*] Nothing to say before you join Emmett, Parnell, and O'Leary? [*Moves closer.*] Christ! [*Waves his hand quickly before* O'RIORDON'S *eyes.*] If this isn't the fiend's own luck! See, boy, he's blind!

2ND TAN: Cor, that's a bit of luck. We can leave him, eh? I'll have a look out of the landing window.

1ST TAN: Dead or alive! Are you forgetting the little posters, boy?

2ND TAN: Here, you ain't going to knock off a blind man, are you?

1ST TAN: Oh, but of course, boy. It might even be a charity to him. [*To* O'RIORDON]: You wouldn't want to stumble your life through, just a bore to your friends, now, would you, Mr O'Riordon, sir? [*Silence.*] You see, boy, we will be

doing him a favour – and, of course, ourselves. All concerned are delighted. You keep guard, watch the drive, and
see that Mr O'Riordon's last moments are undisturbed. [*To*
O'RIORDON]: I do apologize for all this shooting, but there,
it's a lucky man who has a quiet death.

2ND TAN: Here, get it over quick, if you're going to.

1ST TAN: No insubordination, boy. I hate to remind you I'm
your superior officer. After Mr O'Riordon has given us so
much trouble, he can't expect too easy a way out, can he?
That would not be just, and I'm a stickler for justice. And
Mr O'Riordon would be a Catholic, no doubt? I wonder
when he was last at confession. He would like a minute or
two to attempt an act of contrition. Perhaps? Or maybe he
feels safe and might even welcome a temptation or two, at
the last, just to show how strong he is. Let me see – what
are the seven deadly sins? Isn't pride the first? [*Slaps*
O'RIORDON *viciously across the face.*] Prophesy unto us,
O'Riordon, who is he that struck thee?

2ND TAN: Here, we should be doing something about the
fight?

1ST TAN: No, no, we're far more use alive. And I never did
like a hurly-burly. [*Silence.*] So, Mr O'Riordon has no
speech to make. Not a word. Nothing about Erin, Kath-
leen Ni Houlihan, Up the Green Flag? [*Clap of thunder.*]
What does the thunder say, I wonder. But nothing from
you. Well, well, all good things must come to an end, and
life, some say, is a good thing.

2ND TAN: For Gawd's sake let's get out of here. The shooting's stopped – they'll be back.

1ST TAN: So they will. We'd better not use a gun – so noisy.
Cold steel is better, and so much more frightening, Mr
O'Riordon, sir, don't you agree? [*Puts the knife-point on*
O'RIORDON'S *neck.*] So much more frightening.

   [O'RIORDON, *with a great cry, swings to one side, grabs his*
   arm, and with a wrestler's throw hurls the little man over his

head. He lands on his back on the polished table, scattering Shamus's firmament of spoons.]

2ND TAN: 'Ere. [*Grabs* O'RIORDON. *They close and crash to the floor.*]

[1ST TAN *picks himself up.*]

1ST TAN: Hold him still, boy, hold him still. I'll finish him.

[JOHNNY *appears running on the stairs, with a gun.*]

JOHNNY: Stay where you are. Get back to the wall.

[1ST TAN *backs,* 2ND TAN *gets up, backs with him.* O'RIORDON *rises, gropes.*]

JOHNNY: All right, Michael, stay still. [*Goes to* O'RIORDON *and puts him into chair, still covering the* TANS.] Thank God I heard the clatter. Where did these thugs spring from?

O'RIORDON: I don't know at all.

1ST TAN: You're a British officer? Or why are you wearing the coat?

JOHNNY: I am.

1ST TAN: Well, there's luck. Come on, boy, let's be off.

JOHNNY: Stay where you are, and keep your hands up.

1ST TAN: Oh, have you joined the enemy?

JOHNNY: I have no enemies now except the like of you.

1ST TAN: Well, for God's sake, we're sent here to help you do your job. Let us go. They'll be back here any minute.

JOHNNY: Stay where you are. [*They drop their bandoleers.*] Well, Michael, what do you want doing with them? They're your prisoners.

O'RIORDON: Sure, I don't know. What would I be wanting with them? A few minutes of their company nearly lasted me a lifetime as it is.

JOHNNY: No use putting *them* on parole.

1ST TAN: Why not try it? You can't point that gun at us for ever, can you?

2ND TAN: And they'll be back, mate. You wouldn't turn us over to Kelly, would you?

O'RIORDON: Who told you Kelly was here?

1ST TAN: The little birds are on our side, Mr O'Riordon, sir.

O'RIORDON: God, can we never keep a secret! Just blow on our heads and men tell the time by our white thoughts puffed on the wind.

JOHNNY: Well, Michael, what do we do? A pretty problem in loyalty is this.

1ST TAN: There's no problem at all: you let us go. We can't be Mr O'Riordon's prisoners, as he's not any more a soldier, and we can't be yours as you happen to be on our side.

2ND TAN: Come on, mate, they'll be back.

O'RIORDON: Oh, let them go, let them go. Open all cages: even the buzzard has a right to the air. Fly away.

KELLY [off]: Michael!

1ST TAN: Come, boy, on our way. [Hears KELLY'S footsteps outside.] What's that? The other door, quick.

KELLY [entering swiftly and seeing TANS]: What in the name of – Stand still, the both of you. [Covers them.] And how did these slip through my fowler's net?

O'RIORDON: Scouts, I heard them say they were. They must have crossed the river by the old ford.

KELLY [calling off]: Scanlon!

SCANLON [off]: Coming, sir!

KELLY: And what did you all find to talk about while I was away? Who was on whose side?

O'RIORDON: Johnny saved my life.

KELLY [coldly]: So. Captain Tregarthen beat me to the rescue, did he? He seems to have his loyalties mixed.

JOHNNY: I'm on parole: that means I can't fight against you.

KELLY: Doesn't your Army oath mean you can't fight for us?

JOHNNY: Would you rather I'd let Michael be killed? [This sends KELLY into a cold rage.]

[Enter SCANLON.]

KELLY: Two stray birds. See them caged.

SCANLON: Mother of God! How did they get by?

KELLY: I wonder will you ever obey an order without asking questions?

SCANLON: Sorry, sir. But they've just brought Kevin Byrne back from the other side of the bridge. Father John was with him when he died.

[KELLY *stands rigid, the great rage in him almost too much to contain.*]

O'RIORDON [*murmuring*]: Kevin – God rest his soul.

KELLY: Take these two to the lodge. I'll come and question them.

SCANLON: At once, sir. This way, the two of you.

[*Exeunt* SCANLON *and both* TANS.]

SCANLON [*off*]: Hey, Dermot, give me a hand with these.

DERMOT [*off*]: I'll be right with you.

KELLY [*to* JOHNNY]: Has Commandant O'Riordon informed you of your future?

JOHNNY: He has told me –

KELLY: Good.

JOHNNY: But I can't believe that Irishmen would murder prisoners of war.

KELLY: I regret your faith is misplaced. You may call it murder, if it's any consolation. The time is the day after tomorrow, Saturday, at six o'clock in the morning. The place, here. Is that understood?

JOHNNY [*nods*]: Yes.

KELLY: All arrangements will be in my hands, Michael, so you needn't concern yourself. Meanwhile, Captain Tregarthen remains your prisoner.

O'RIORDON: Sean –

KELLY: Now I must question the Captain's two friends, then take my report to Headquarters. A success, I suppose. I wonder if Kevin Byrne's wife will think so.

[*During the last few speeches* MOLLY *has entered to the top of the stairs. As* KELLY *turns, he sees her. They hold eyes for a moment, then* KELLY *swiftly goes.*]

MOLLY: Michael, darling –

O'RIORDON: Molly –

JOHNNY: Molly, I told you not to follow me.

MOLLY: Michael, is it true? Mother of God, it can't be true!

O'RIORDON: Johnny, you didn't tell her?

JOHNNY: I had to –

MOLLY: Sure, of course he had to. I knew something terrible
    was creeping up on us all when you sent me away. Michael
    what can we do at all? Isn't Kelly your friend? Won't he
    do as you ask?

O'RIORDON: Yes, Sean Kelly is my friend, and he'd do any-
    thing in God's world for me if 'twas only himself concerned.
    But sure, orders are not in his power to change, or so he'll
    say.

MOLLY: But if you ask him –

O'RIORDON: No, Molly, I know what he'd say. 'Leave it to
    me, Michael,' he'd say, 'and don't fret yourself.' He always
    had that queer protective feeling all through our fighting
    days. Now, of course, it's worse. He knows what's to be
    done and takes the weight of it off me. His kind of kindness
    will kill us all.

MOLLY: Then what'll we do at all?

O'RIORDON: Look to ourselves for the answer. We must get
    Johnny away between us.

JOHNNY: But Michael, you heard what Kelly said. I'm your
    prisoner. There's still my parole. Surely there must be an
    appeal against this?

O'RIORDON: For God's sake forget the parole. You can't let
    a web of words catch you like a fly, and be killed; and an
    appeal, I can tell you, is a waste of time. The murder of
    M'Gill, O'Shea, and Keogh will keep the Army at the
    point of fury for weeks. It's ourselves only can help us.

MOLLY: Johnny, love, don't be a dear fool. Isn't your parole
    given to Michael, and, sure, he can give it back.

O'RIORDON: And I do. That's a first wedding present.

JOHNNY: But Michael, what about the third name? If not mine, it'll be another's.

O'RIORDON: Johnny, you can't let yourself be killed because someone else *may* die if you don't. That's out of our hands. Except we can pray to God no one else will suffer. But your safety and your life and your love is in our hands, so let's not talk or talk'll be the death of us.

JOHNNY: You know it's not as easy as that, Michael, and I can well see if you were in my position what you would do.

O'RIORDON: Sure, I'd be gone by now.

JOHNNY: You wouldn't. You'd do as I do. I know you, Michael. You'd be proud that your parole held you stronger than bars. You'd escape from a prison, but not from your word, would you?

O'RIORDON: Holy God, Johnny, what are you making out of me? As Christ is my judge, I'd ride for the border and be damned to anyone who tried to stop me.

MOLLY: I've been thinking of ways and means while you two were talking. Now listen to me. There'll be no argument. Johnny and I are going to England at once.

JOHNNY: Molly –

MOLLY: The only question is, how is it best to be done. [*To* JOHNNY.] We'd jump out of the way if the wind was blowing a tree on the top of us, and there's no difference at all now. Michael, how's it to be done? Could Johnny ride off at once.

JOHNNY: Not now. The stables'll be under guard since the fight. There'll be a few Tans about yet.

MOLLY: Would the railway do?

O'RIORDON: The station'll be guarded too, I'd say.

MOLLY: Couldn't he board the train on the slope, where it slows down, you know, a little way beyond the station?

O'RIORDON: He could do that –

MOLLY: The goods train, Michael, that's it! The goods train

that passes to-morrow early, about six. And old Tim, the guard, has known me since first I could walk. He'll do anything for me. I tell you what, now – Listen, Johnny. I'll go south to Castledown by this evening's train, find old Tim and tell him I'm coming north with him in the morning, and as much else as he needs to know.

JOHNNY: Darling.

MOLLY: And you, Johnny, can join me on the slope beyond the station at six to-morrow morning. I'll get the driver – it'll be Barney Doonan, he's Tim's mate – to slow down to a walking pace on the slope. It may cost me a bit.

O'RIORDON: Ah, sure, half-a-crown in the slot will open his conscience.

MOLLY: And we'll give a signal, Johnny, to tell you all's well and I'm aboard. Three whistles, we'll make it – three whistles – and as soon as you hear them, you jump aboard the guard's van, and there Tim'll have a cup of tea for you and me.

O'RIORDON: That's a fine scheme. And I'll look after this end. I'll discreetly find out who's on sentry-go at the time Johnny'll have to leave, and see he gets away. If it's Dermot Fone we'll be all right, and I think 'tis him. I heard him moan about the dawn guard. If I have to, I'll use my authority, but we'll try to meet with no one. Sean Kelly'll be away. He's going to-day to report to H.Q. and won't be back, at the soonest, before to-morrow noon. And by then you'll be clean away on the road to Belfast. Something's happened to me – I'm thinking kindly of Belfast!

MOLLY [*laughing with an edge of hysteria*]: God bless you, Michael, God bless you. Oh, now the world looks clear again! God spin the world over quickly and let to-morrow come!

O'RIORDON: You know, sometimes I think in my darkness I can stretch my arms up and read the stars like a page of Braille, and the future in them. Shall I try now?

MOLLY: Yes, do!

O'RIORDON: Can't reach.

[*They laugh.* O'RIORDON *drops his hands, touches a remaining spoon on the table, casually fingers it.*]

MOLLY: Well, Johnny, why so gloomy? Wake up, darling, wake up to life.

JOHNNY: Michael, what can I do? I – I'm still haunted by the thought of that third name. And won't this escape land you in serious trouble?

O'RIORDON: Saints alive, man, are you mad or what? To stay on, I tell you, is suicide itself. If death's what you want out of life, you'll wait for Sean to come back. If life's what you want, you'll go! I'm sorry, Johnny, I know how you feel. Yes, I'd feel the same way myself. But you can bet your last shilling I'd let myself be persuaded! So come on, Johnny, be persuaded. Swim with the tide, come on. I'll be in no trouble when you're gone, so don't fret.

MOLLY: Johnny, love, this is the only favour I'll ever ask you all our lives. Come on the train, will you, love, come on the train.

JOHNNY [*after a pause, unhappily*]: All right.

O'RIORDON: Well, there's nothing like good news to make a man unhappy! Go on, Molly, lift some of Tolly's whiskey from the sideboard. We'll toast ourselves and cheer up Johnny.

MOLLY: So we will. [*Snatches whiskey and glasses.*] Here you are, Johnny, something to cheer you up. There's nothing can go wrong now. Will you not be the Senior Officer, Michael, when Kelly's away.

O'RIORDON: I will.

MOLLY: Well, then, there's nothing to fear. Here you are, Michael. [*Gives drink.*] Here's to to-morrow and the Belfast goods train.

[*They drink.*]

O'RIORDON: Ah, sure, that's good. Little Tolly has a fine

H

taste in whiskey and it's no lie. More. [MOLLY *pours*.] And
here's to the mailboat from Belfast to Liverpool.

    [*They drink.*]

MOLLY: Now, Johnny, feeling better?

JOHNNY: I feel as though my head was three feet above my
shoulders. What's in that bottle?

O'RIORDON: Only good Irish whiskey. Give him some more.

JOHNNY: And here's to the farm on Broome Hill.

MOLLY: Yes.

O'RIORDON: That's to be your home, is it? Well, God send
it great love and joy. [*They drink.*] Do you know, I've
never got drunk before in so short a time. Excitement and
whiskey will send the best of us under the table. And Holy
God, I've had no lunch! Well, here we go! [*Swigs back the
last of his drink, and sings very fast a verse of 'The Palatine's
Daughter', then stops suddenly.*] God, we must be crazy!
Sean'll be back. Get out of sight, the two of you. Put
away the drink. [MOLLY *does so*.] This'd be queer conduct for the likes of us. Molly, you'd better be harnessing
the trap to catch the train. And don't let the two of you be
seen together by Sean.

MOLLY: We won't. Maybe we'd better be saying good-bye
now. Good-bye, Michael darling, thank you for all. [*Kisses
him lightly. To* JOHNNY]: Until to-morrow morning,
dearest. Three whistles of a train will sing in our ears till
our dying day as the sign of a great deliverance. God bless
you, love, and be careful.

JOHNNY: I will. [*They kiss.*]

MOLLY: Soon we'll be saying 'I will' with a difference. [*She
goes to the door.*] Tim'll drive the trap back when the train's
gone. [*She runs suddenly to* JOHNNY – *a long, desperate kiss –
then she runs out.*]

    [JOHNNY *watches her from the window. Pause. He sits down
    desolate, suddenly puts his head in his hands.*]

JOHNNY: It's a long time.

O'RIORDON: A short night only.

JOHNNY: Stop me thinking, Michael, or I'll not be responsible for what I do. I've never been so afraid.

O'RIORDON: Now, don't be fretting yourself. I tell you what we'll do. You come and lie on the couch in my room to-night. We'll sleep by turns and watch by turns till half after five. Then I'll see you clear of the gates and you'll be free. It's as simple as that. Kelly's away – he won't be back till noon, and by then you'll be out of the shadow. We'll play chess, maybe, to kill time.

JOHNNY: Yes, let's do that. I'm afraid, Michael, just blind funk. My heart's going like a hammer and I'm cold all over – Christ! –

O'RIORDON: Let you not be worrying. You'll laugh at this to-morrow, and you'll be another man entirely. Time'll quieten you. Just sit still and let the hours slide through you soft as sand, and before you know it the morning will be on us. Now you'd better keep clear till Kelly's away. He'll be going soon. Go to my room and I'll join you. Better we shouldn't be seen talking. And I think I hear Kelly coming back – off with you.

JOHNNY: Sorry for the outburst.

O'RIORDON: Away with you, quick.

[JOHNNY *goes upstairs.*]

[MICHAEL *sits quiet.*]

[*Enter* KELLY *and* SCANLON.]

KELLY: A very unpleasant gentleman, the smaller of your guests, Michael.

O'RIORDON: He was that.

KELLY: And no pleasanter when I left him. Oh, a little subdued. The other was just a thick.

SCANLON: Ah, they was a pagan couple, a pagan couple.

KELLY [*coming upon the glasses on the sideboard, in one of which some whiskey is left*]: Early in the day to be drinking, Michael.

O'RIORDON: Well, the Tans shook me up.

KELLY: And you left one poured out for me. That's thought-ful. God bless us. [*He drinks.*] I'm off at five o'clock, Michael, I'll be back to-morrow.

O'RIORDON: Will you see the General?

KELLY: He should be there, yes.

O'RIORDON: Then will you do a thing for me?

KELLY: I will, of course. What?

O'RIORDON: Ask him for clemency for Johnny.

KELLY: I'll ask. But, Michael, I hold out no hope, none at all. You know the General.

O'RIORDON: Yes, I know him. But ask, will you – promise.

KELLY: I promise, but it's waste of breath. For God's sake don't build up hope.

O'RIORDON: No, I won't. I won't. I'll go and lie down, I think. I don't feel good at all. See you to-morrow, Sean.

KELLY: To-morrow, Michael. [*Exit* O'RIORDON.] Michael's taking it hard.

SCANLON: Taking what hard, Chief?

KELLY: Is there nothing you'll understand in one? Sentence of death on Captain Tregarthen.

SCANLON: Does he know him, or what?

KELLY: He's only been under Michael's charge for three months.

SCANLON: Mother of God, is it the fellow here? Then are we going through with it? [*Hastily*]: Yes, yes, of course. That's ill luck, ill luck.

KELLY: Have you forgotten Keogh, M'Gill, and O'Shea? And have you forgotten Kevin Byrne? – Kevin Byrne! [*He sweeps the last of the spoons to the floor in a spasm of cold rage.*] Why in the name of God did it have to be him? Do I have to be left when the last of my friends is dead?

SCANLON [*shyly*]: I'm still with you, sir.

KELLY [*ignoring him*]: There's only Michael left, and him a cripple. All my love's on him now, and there's nothing under God's sun'll not be done for him. [*To himself*]: Now, Michael, what do you want most in life? I know. I'll give you that, by God, I'll give you that, though I lose your love for ever. [*Pause.*] But at all costs he must be spared being there at the execution.

SCANLON: Yes, sir. Is it fond of the Englishman he is?

KELLY [*ignoring the question*]: I've told him it's fixed for Saturday morning, so Michael will expect it then. Instead, I suppose, we'll have to bring it forward. Make it to-morrow. Yes, we'll make it to-morrow. I'll come back early, before Michael is up. Tregarthen's room is the other side of the house from his, so he'll not know till it's all over. Yes. That's the way it'll have to be.

SCANLON: Sure, that's hard on the Englishman. Will he want to see the priest?

KELLY: He'll be given time for last messages and the rest. But he'll not be allowed to see Michael, so Michael'll be spared what must happen. He'll simply know it's been done.

SCANLON: It's hard on the Englishman.

KELLY [*coldly*]: Only Michael matters. It's higher orders than ours condemned Tregarthen. [*To himself*]: And other reasons – other reasons.

SCANLON: Other reasons, sir?

KELLY [*looking straight at him for the first time*]: Are you the only one that's with me? That's loneliness all right.

SCANLON: What's that, sir?

KELLY: No matter. I return to-morrow, early, is that understood? I'll bring a firing squad with me. You need not detail anyone from here. Captain Tregarthen will be wakened when I come and told of the change of plan. Now I must go to Headquarters.

SCANLON: What time shall I expect you, Chief?

KELLY: Oh, some time before six. Detail an escort for the two Tan prisoners.

SCANLON: I will, sir. And I'll be up to meet you to-morrow.

[SCANLON *waits an eager moment for a possible word of commendation.* KELLY *looks at him with eyes like stones.*]

[*Exit* SCANLON. KELLY *waits and looks a long moment where* O'RIORDON *has gone.*]

[*Enter* SHAMUS. *Does not see* KELLY *but sees the scattered spoons.*]

SHAMUS: Holy God, who's knocked the stars from the sky?

CURTAIN

ACT THREE

Next morning, about 5.30. Stage dark.

> [*Enter from outside* FIRST SENTRY. *He opens the curtains.
> Strong moonlight and a little help from the coming dawn flood
> in. Enter* SECOND SENTRY *sleepily.*]

1ST SOLDIER: Oh, Dermot, are you after getting up at last?
D'you know it's ten minutes since I shook you.

2ND SOLDIER: Oh, is that all? Sure, what's ten minutes
weighed in the scales of eternity?

1ST SOLDIER: Weighed in the scales of a night guard, 'tis a
bloody long time. Scanlon's up and waiting at the bridge
for you! Get out there and let me hit the hay.

2ND SOLDIER: Listen!

1ST SOLDIER: What is it? I don't hear a thing.

2ND SOLDIER: The very first bird awake. Scanlon? What's
he doing up and infecting the morning air? Can't he sleep at
all while his beloved Kelly's away?

1ST SOLDIER: Hell, the sun's on his way. That means I'll not
get to sleep. Why in the name of God can't you get up
when you're called?

2ND SOLDIER: Sloth, dear man, just sloth. A man can't have
all the gifts and bounding out of bed isn't one of mine. Me
and the rooster are the last up always.

1ST SOLDIER: Well, I'm for bed. There's nothing doing out
there.

2ND SOLDIER: Have ye ever noticed how lazy the rooster is?
At the first break in the night ye hear the first bird turn
over and cheep sleepily, and he's joined by others and others
till the whole choir are wide awake and singing for the
deliverance of daylight. Then up at last gets the rooster and

scares them all with a noise as sharp as a shower of bullets. Shot at dawn they are, by a fusillade of sound from the gun-barrel throat of a red bird.

1ST SOLDIER: Ye'd better come and talk me to sleep. I'll need help.

2ND SOLDIER: No one sleeps when I talk. It's the Gift, man, it's the Gift.

1ST SOLDIER: Well, good-night and a quiet guard.

2ND SOLDIER: Good-morning. It'll be a noisy guard, for sure, with the hopeful birds rising and the rooster at the last.
    [*Exit* 1ST SENTRY. 2ND SENTRY – *he is* DERMOT FONE, O'RIORDON'S *friend, a Western Islander – looks out of the window a long moment, turns lazily, hums: 'Will ye lend me your wife for an hour and a quarter, O, the brown and the yellow ale.' He has his hand on the door.*]

O'RIORDON [*from the top of the stairs, whispers*]: Dermot.

DERMOT: Michael! For God's sake, can't ye sleep or what?

O'RIORDON: Dermot, is anyone about?

DERMOT: No, Phelim's just hit the hay.

O'RIORDON: Can I have your help?

DERMOT: Ye can of course. Ye've only to ask. It's help to get your friend Tregarthen away, I suppose?

O'RIORDON: God help us, are my thoughts that clear on my face?

DERMOT: Only to me, Michael darlin'. I was wondering how long it would be before you'd ask me. Ssh! Stop breathing a minute. No – I thought it was Phelim coming back, though why he should, God knows. Sure, his bed's the only strong love of his life. What can I do?

O'RIORDON [*calling softly upstairs*]: Johnny! – [JOHNNY *comes down.*] This is Dermot Fone – he'll help us. Didn't I say he would?

DERMOT: Ah, sure, we've shuttled our greetings across the lawn before now, and this morning will make us old friends.

JOHNNY: Yes, and thank you.

DERMOT: For nothing at all. It'll give me delight to foil Sean Kelly. I can't think why you love him, Michael. A man who's never wrong is a great menace to all his friends.

O'RIORDON: Can we go now, Dermot? This night's waiting was nearly the end of us.

DERMOT: Ye can, of course. O, wait. Scanlon, said Phelim, is waiting on the bridge.

O'RIORDON: Scanlon! In the name of God, what's he doing up?

DERMOT [*satirically*]: Making sure, I suppose, he's in time for Kelly's arrival this afternoon.

JOHNNY: Is there no other way but the bridge?

O'RIORDON: No, none.

DERMOT: But don't fear, I'll get him away. Up towards the beech wood, that'll be safe.

JOHNNY: We can't leave till you do. He'll see every move from the bridge.

DERMOT: Don't fret now – I'll spin a noose of words and lead him away acquiescent as an ox.

O'RIORDON: How long'll ye be? The train's due in half an hour.

DERMOT: Give me ten minutes, and the way'll be clear for ye. Scanlon's no man to withstand the Gift. And God go with ye, Tregarthen, even so far as England.

JOHNNY: And with you. Thanks.

[*Exit* DERMOT.]

JOHNNY: Ten minutes!

O'RIORDON: O, the straws and the camel's back! A minute's a straw only, and yesterday it was light on the wind as a summer fly. Now it's a hundredweight of heavy waiting.

JOHNNY: It's cold, too.

O'RIORDON: It'll be a while yet before we feel the summer. And half past five in the morning is a cold-hearted hour. It was kind of God to ordain we should be asleep now, with the comfort of dreams.

JOHNNY: Yes, and it's an hour that drains your courage away, have you noticed? During the war, I know, I suffered all kinds of terrors at this hour that the daylight – or even the honest ghosts of midnight – would never allow near me.

O'RIORDON: Sure, every hour has its own attendant spirit, and this not a genial one. [*Brightly, to cheer* JOHNNY]: A while ago, I remember, I invented a new kind of a clock, and each hour was called not by the humdrum numbers, ye know, but by *name* – the hour of the bee, for instance, or the hour of the swan, or the owl. This hour, as I recall, was the hour of the Demon.

JOHNNY: Tell me about your clock, to pass the time.

O'RIORDON: No better way! Well, 'twas altogether a lovely notion. Ye see, the clock face was to be of two enamel circles, one inside the other.

JOHNNY: Yes?

O'RIORDON: One of black enamel on the inside, for the hours of the night, and one in white enamel on the outside for the hours of the day.

JOHNNY: But the hours of daylight vary with the time of the year.

O'RIORDON: For God's sake, Johnny, don't be so Protestant! I'm telling you, this was not at all supposed to be a lovely *clock* – just a lovely *idea* for a clock!

JOHNNY: Oh, I see. And why was daylight on the outside?

O'RIORDON: Well, and why not? I was younger then, and looked on the brighter side. Anyway, instead of marking the hours by figures, as if magical time itself were a matter for dull arithmetic, they were each to be marked by a little coloured enamel *picture* – of an owl or a peacock or a dragon or whatever the hour was called. Ye see? Wouldn't that have looked a fine thing on the mantelpiece?

JOHNNY: It would. Come on, tell me about the hours, to fill the minutes.

O'RIORDON: I can't remember the whole. Midday was the

hour of the tiger, because it was strong and sleepy and had its hot yellow light striped by the cold black shadows.

JOHNNY: Bravo. I bet all your hours weren't as good as that one.

O'RIORDON: Well, no. But seven or eight in the evening was the hour of the swan, I remember. For a swan's always more of a swan in the evening, don't you think?

JOHNNY: Oh, much more. With the stars above him and the stars below him, like a quiet white ship.

O'RIORDON: Or like a king of two firmaments.

JOHNNY: Or like a swan!

O'RIORDON [laughing]: Yes.

JOHNNY: And this was the hour of the Demon?

O'RIORDON: Yes. The hour of the Demon. What's the time?

JOHNNY: Not five minutes gone yet.

O'RIORDON: The Demon moves slowly; where's his wings?

JOHNNY: Oh, I wish it was the hour of the swan to-morrow. No, to-day. That will go faster than a swan ever flew. Ssssss! – I want to stamp about, it's so cold. Michael, what was that ballad you sang once, about the swan in the evening?

O'RIORDON: 'She moved through the fair.'

JOHNNY: Yes. Hum it to me now quietly. It was lovely.

O'RIORDON: Glory be, I'll sound like an old bull-frog at this hour. The Demon won't like singing, ye know.

JOHNNY: To hell with him! The birds have started, so why shouldn't you?

O'RIORDON: Well, to pass the time. [Sings]:
My young love said to me: My mother won't mind,
And my father won't slight you for lack of kind;
And she stepped away from me, and this she did say:
It will not be long, love, till our wedding day.*

JOHNNY [half to himself]: Not long, love!

O'RIORDON: God, it is cold! Look, Johnny, there's always

* Adapted from an old ballad by Padraic Colum.

tea on the hob for the sentries, just through the door there. Let's both have a cup. Go softly.

JOHNNY: Yes, let's.

[*Exit* JOHNNY. MICHAEL *moves his arms to warm himself, then stiffens. Enter* PHELIM *in his socks.*]

PHELIM: For God's sake, Michael, are ye not well?

O'RIORDON: Phelim! Yes, yes, I'm well. Just couldn't sleep. Go back to bed now.

PHELIM: Will I not get ye a cup of tea, maybe?

O'RIORDON: No, no. Er – Dermot's getting me one now.

PHELIM: Jasus, isn't he the lazy lout? Up late, and no sooner up than supping tea! Ye'd think his bed was a woman, he's that loath to leave it. Are ye sure, now, there's nothing I can do for ye?

O'RIORDON: No, no, nothing. I'll maybe go for a walk with Dermot. Go to bed now. Good-night and God bless you.

PHELIM: Good-night and God bless you, Michael.

[*Exit* PHELIM.]

O'RIORDON [*softly*]: Christ.

JOHNNY [*from the other door*]: Don't worry, he's gone.

O'RIORDON: Yes, and he won't come back. Dermot and I swap songs at all hours of the day and night: he won't think it strange.

JOHNNY [*handing steaming cup of tea*]: Here, get this into you, it's wonderful.

O'RIORDON [*drinks*]: Ah, yes.

JOHNNY: Do you remember that marvellous pot of tea Molly made yesterday morning?

O'RIORDON: Yes, the first tea we ever drank in the new-created world – wasn't it? – a toast to the beginning.

JOHNNY: This tastes good, too.

O'RIORDON: Yes. What's the time?

JOHNNY: Seven and a half minutes.

O'RIORDON: Dear God! When will it end?

JOHNNY: Will Dermot manage?

O'RIORDON: For sure he will. I'd trust him with my life and more.

JOHNNY: Well, let's have the rest of the song. It'll fill the great empty minutes. Your throat's warmer now.

O'RIORDON: The next verse has your swan in the lake. It goes – [*Sings*]:
"She stepped away from me and she moved through the fair
  And fondly I watched her move here and move there,
  And then she went homeward, with one star awake,
  As the swan in the evening moves over the lake."
[*Suddenly*]: What was that?

JOHNNY: I heard nothing.

O'RIORDON: It sounded like the owl call Dermot uses sometimes for a warning. Listen.

JOHNNY: Nothing. Perhaps it was a real owl.

O'RIORDON: Yes, maybe.

JOHNNY [*at the window*]: I see nothing. [*Looking at watch.*] Another minute yet. I suppose we'd better give Dermot his ten.

O'RIORDON: Yes, we must.

JOHNNY: The last verse, and it'll be time to go.

O'RIORDON [*sings*]:
  Last night she came to me, my dead love came in:
  So softly she came that her feet made no din.
  [*Stops suddenly.*] Sorry, I thought I heard it again. [*Sings.*]
  And she laid her hand on me, and this she did say:
  It will not be long, love, till our wedding day.
  [*Rises suddenly and turns to the door. It opens quietly.*
  KELLY *stands there with* SCANLON. *Kelly puts his hands on*
  O'RIORDON'S *shoulders, who gives a great cry.*]

KELLY: Michael, I'm sorry you're up. I was coming softly so as not to wake you.

O'RIORDON: What are you doing back? What are you doing back? This afternoon you said – This afternoon. Johnny, am

I going mad? For God's sake, is it Kelly here, or am I
going mad?

KELLY: Yes, Michael, it's Kelly here.

O'RIORDON: What d'ye mean, coming back like a nightmare on the fringe of day? Dear God, I'm lost surely –
Johnny, why don't you speak? Are you with me or not?
No, don't answer. God let this be a nightmare! Let me
wake up! Let me wake up and know Johnny's at watch by
the bed, and it's time to be gone!

KELLY: You're broad awake, Michael, and I'm sorry you are,
for I've bad news for your friend. I had thought you'd be
asleep and be spared the knowing. For I passed on your plea
for clemency; I'm afraid it was refused. [*Formally to*
JOHNNY]: I have here a warrant of execution, signed by
high authority and entrusted to me. The time named here
is the dawn of Friday, April the third. [*A frozen pause.*]

JOHNNY: Friday? But to-day is Friday –

KELLY: Friday is to-day, and dawn is very soon.

O'RIORDON: Sean, you're mad surely. What do you torture
us for? I was here and heard you say it. Saturday you said –
Saturday. And Saturday is to-morrow.

KELLY: I know. But the warrant says Friday, and Friday is to-
day. It's regrettable, but it must be carried out according
to the orders in the warrant.

O'RIORDON [*helplessly*]: But – I –

KELLY [*to* JOHNNY]: Outside with us, there's a priest and a
parson of the Anglican persuasion. Do you want to see
either? [*No answer.*] Do you want to see either?

JOHNNY: Either?

KELLY: The priest or the minister. Do you want to see either?

JOHNNY: No –

SCANLON [*gently*]: Maybe later ye will.

KELLY: Meanwhile you may have time for any last messages
you may want to write. We'll see they're delivered. I
suggest you retire to another room. Scanlon, will you

escort Captain Tregarthen and see he has everything he asks for.

SCANLON: I will, sir. Will ye go with me? Please, sir.

[*Exeunt* SCANLON *and* JOHNNY, *who seems stunned.*]

O'RIORDON [*after a pause*]: Sean.

KELLY: Yes.

O'RIORDON: Is there no one else in the room?

KELLY: No one.

O'RIORDON: Just you and me?

KELLY: Just you and me.

O'RIORDON: Sean, I don't know why you've played this terrible trick on us. Does even God know why? It's bitter cruel to cut off hope like this.

KELLY: In this case, Michael, there never was hope. I told you that.

O'RIORDON: Oh, but there was! There was! And there is! I'll not give up hope, never!

KELLY: Don't torture yourself more, Michael. You've suffered enough.

O'RIORDON: We've all suffered enough, Sean. All of us. Why do we need to suffer more? It's in your power to save us. One word from you and Johnny can escape death. I can escape a heavier sorrow than my eyes' loss. And yourself, Sean, can escape the remorse of it all, the terrible remorse of it all. And this time you'll feel it, Sean! You may pretend that so far in your life you've never felt it, but now you'll feel it! Now, if never before, you'll feel the remorse!

KELLY: Perhaps I will at last. That's part of the price, I suppose.

O'RIORDON: Price? For what, in the name of God?

KELLY: I can't answer you that, Michael.

O'RIORDON: Sean, you can't know the power you've got in your one word. Johnny and Molly were to be married, did you know that?

KELLY: I'd guessed it.

O'RIORDON: And I was aiding him just now to escape – did you know that?

KELLY: I'd guessed that, too.

O'RIORDON: And at this moment Molly is on the morning train that is due to pass here in fifteen minutes. At this moment, Sean! Carrying such a burden of hope and love as would crack a smaller heart. She is to give a signal of three whistles from the engine and Johnny was to jump the train on the slope. And the two were to sail in safety to England. That was the plan, Sean. And now, because you've taken a whim to come back this morning instead of this afternoon, all the generations, the children and the grandchildren, stretching to God knows what moment of happy time, are holding their breath, to know whether or not they're to be born at all. Are they? A word from you – one word – and they'll live. Or a word the other way, and they'll never be. That's the power of your single word. It's God-like, Sean. You can give life. [KELLY *does not answer.*] Sean! Where are you?

KELLY: Here.

O'RIORDON: And more are waiting than just Johnny for your answer. Molly is waiting. Johnny's father's waiting. And I'm waiting. And I ask you, out of whatever love you may have had for me – and I know that it's been great – that you will turn your head the other way and allow Johnny to go.

KELLY: It's not fair to turn all the blame of decision on me, Michael. In war – and this, remember, is war – who dies? Usually we do not know. We – you and I have done it together – we sight our rifles and we pull the trigger, and how can we know whose heart the bullet will find. That's God's business. We are given orders and we obey them. The pathetic backgrounds of those we kill are normally not visible. There's only one difference now – the background *is* visible. Our duty is not thereby excused, only made harder.

O'RIORDON: But it's not the same. In war, it's kill or be killed. The blood is hot, and God, we hope, will forgive us. Now the blood is cold, and if we kill 'tis without passion, and where is the mercy of God can soften the malice of that? Sean, I know you to be a creature of iron custom, maybe that's what makes you so marvellous a soldier; custom has a harder hold on you than most. I remember only yesterday you saying you'd not been for ten years to the Sacraments and you couldn't break the custom.

You've lived, for all your manhood, in the armour of custom, and you've not once thrown it off to disobey an order you've thought unjust. But sure, customs must be broken some time or they'll kill your mind and make a stone of your heart.

Tell me, now, and answer me truly: what sleep would you lose, and what harm would fall on you if you let Johnny go? Suppose now you'd come back just half an hour later, or suppose we had gone just half an hour earlier – you would simply have shrugged and smiled, maybe, and sent a report to Headquarters that the bird had flown. What is there now to stop you giving me the only thing I've ever asked of you and ever will ask of you? In the name of God and in the name of love – my friend's life.

KELLY: If it were so simple, Michael, I might not hesitate. I'd break more than a custom for you – am in fact doing so, if you knew it. But you're sick, Michael, and you cannot know as well as I what is best for you now.

O'RIORDON: I don't want what is *best* for me! Who knows that, anyway, but God? I, nor you, can see no further than this moment of time, with you and me here in this room; Johnny above, writing, and Molly on the train measuring her heartbeats by the beat of the wheels that are bringing her northward. I see no further than only that. And I know that the next few minutes can shatter or transfigure at least four human lives. And you talk, like a doctor, of sickness –

what is best for me! Best for *me*! Sure, mine is the least
important of the four futures that are waiting on your
word. Mine's a dark one, surely, and must be. Will you put
the light out for the others, too?

KELLY: You're the only one who matters to me, Michael, and
such pain as you're suffering now you're giving yourself.
There was a torture once indulged in, say the novelists, by
our less amiable fellow-Catholics of the Inquisition – the
torture of hope. The doors of the cell were left open, the
prisoner miraculously took himself through corridors, past
guards, to the mysteriously open main gate to freedom,
only to be met on the threshold by the Chief Inquisitor,
bathed in reproachful tears. You, too, Michael, are tor-
tured by hope, but I have opened no doors, left no corridors
unguarded, no gates wide; I have made it plain what must
happen, knowing that to be less cruel. You are torturing
yourself.

O'RIORDON: But, Sean, there are things in this I can't at all
understand. You said a minute or two ago that you would
break more than a custom for me, and in the same breath
you say you will not. Talk about what is best for me. I cannot at all see how I am involved, except as a friend of theirs
and a friend of yours. And if you go through with this, I
lose you all, Johnny, Molly – and you, Sean. I lose you!

KELLY: I know. [*A spasm of pain.*]

O'RIORDON: Yet you'll not save me from that – if it's only
me you're thinking of?

KELLY: Michael, you may think me cold-hearted. In a way I
am. I don't suffer as others do from remorse and yearning.
But I know what and who I love, and I am constant.
Always we've been especially close, and since you've been
in the dark I've used my eyes for you. They can see now
what is the best way for you. You have to trust me, Michael,
whether you want to or not. You've always loved others
too much to have a lot to spare for yourself. You would

always do what was best for *them*. But now that I'm in control of things, it's going this time at least to be the other way.

O'RIORDON: I don't understand you, Sean, I don't understand you –

KELLY: Love wears many masks, Michael. Look round you: your friend's is wearing the conventional mask – of romance; yours is wearing what could be called maybe a mask of renouncement. Perhaps one day, when you're happy, you'll see behind the devil's mask mine is wearing now.

O'RIORDON: But how can I ever be happy? You don't understand what you are doing. You think everyone feels as you do. My love is wearing no mask. Renouncement? – What do you mean? It's no noble renouncement, no brave gesture to cover a broken heart, that I'm after making. You talk as though I'd be a happy man if only I could marry Molly. If that's what you're thinking, Sean, in the name of God, believe me, you're wrong. My happiness now is bound up with Johnny and Molly, with the *both* of them. Do you understand? – The both of them. My only happiness in life is the reflection of theirs, and 'tis beautiful because of it.

KELLY: You're talking from the darkness, Michael. I can see. And outside the light is gathering – it'll be dawn soon.

O'RIORDON: You can see more in the dark than if you're blinded with light. Sean, the time is going, and I – I don't know at all what to say. O God, help me, words don't seem any more to mean what they did. I've told you, you'll bring my life about me like a dark tower blown down by a wind that always till now was soft and friendly. You answer me flatly it will not. How can I reach you, Sean? Don't shut me out from you. How can you see the agony in me, and how can you bear to see it and not speak the word to take it away?

KELLY: You're thinking only of this moment. I'm thinking

of your whole life. Shared sorrow is a strong bond. Accept what will happen, Michael, don't let hope intrude. Hope will just vex you, it cannot help. If there's one thing certain in this coming day it is that Captain John Tregarthen will die. Once you have accepted that, the quick agony will cease and time will do the rest. I'm trying to ease your pain by taking hope away.

O'RIORDON [*brokenly*]: But I love him – I love him –

KELLY: There's the rooster. It's time. The sun's just touching the top of the beech wood.

O'RIORDON: And I had thought for years that you were my friend. For what's a friend, in the name of Christ, if he won't say one word to save another from death and me from lifelong sorrow? Is it nothing that I must hate you for ever for this? By God, if I had my eyes I'd tear your heart out living! What a coward you've turned out to be at the last, vaunting yourself over a blind beggar, for that's all I am now surely – a blind beggar crying for the pence of pity and coming home with an empty bowl.

KELLY [*gently putting his revolver in* O'RIORDON'S *hand – quietly*]: My head is in point-blank range. When I am gone, you are the senior officer.

O'RIORDON [*aghast, not tempted*]: I can't – I can't.

KELLY: You're not in cold blood: touch my head here, so you will not miss. [*Gently, taking back the revolver*]: You see, Michael, it's not easy to carry the decisions of life and death. Let me take the burden for you.

[*Enter* JOHNNY *and* SCANLON.]

O'RIORDON: Is it –

JOHNNY [*giving him two letters*]: These – deliver –

O'RIORDON: Yes.

KELLY: Is there anything else you wish to say?

JOHNNY: To you, no.

[*Throughout the following scene* O'RIORDON *holds the white paper of the letters over his heart.*]

SCANLON: Are you sure, now, you'd not like to see the priest?

JOHNNY: Don't be anxious about me. I'm not anxious about you.

SCANLON: No, sir. [*Ashamed.*]

KELLY [*giving a square of white paper to* SCANLON – *quietly*]: This over the heart.

[SCANLON *fumbles to pin the paper over* JOHNNY'S *heart. Puts it too low.*]

JOHNNY [*very quietly*]: My heart is higher than that.

SCANLON [*adjusting it*]: I'm sorry, sir. I'm sorry, sir.

O'RIORDON: Oh, Johnny, I tried, I tried –

JOHNNY: Yes, I know.

KELLY: Shall we go? They are waiting this side of the beech-wood.

JOHNNY: Good-bye, Michael. Thank you for great happiness.

O'RIORDON [*brokenly*]: Johnny – Johnny!

[*Exeunt* SCANLON *and* JOHNNY. KELLY *stays looking a long moment at* O'RIORDON, *then exit.*]

O'RIORDON [*after seconds*]: Sean! Sean!

[*From the distance, three train whistles sound.*]

O'RIORDON: Oh, Christ, my Saviour, what is happening in the light?

[*From outside the orders to aim and fire are heard, followed by a fusillade.* O'RIORDON *stands crumpled, the white paper of the letters still over his heart.*]

[*From the distance come three longer whistles, like the cries of a woman, during the third of which*

SLOW CURTAIN

DONAGH MACDONAGH

Step-in-the-Hollow

To Niall and Barbara

STEP-IN-THE-HOLLOW

This play was first presented at the Gaiety Theatre, Dublin, on 11 March 1957, with the following cast:

MOLLY NOLAN	Una Collins
MICHAEL NEWSOME	Leo Leyden
JAMES STAPLE	Liam Gaffney
JULIA O'SULLIVAN	Pauline Delaney
TEAZIE	Finola O'Shannon
REDMOND O'HANLON	Hilton Edwards
SEÁN O'FENETIC	Norman Rodway
ARGUS O'HONE	Christopher Casson
DANIEL O'CONNELL	Paul Farrell
CRILLY DUFFY	Patrick Bedford
MARGARET MARY ALLEN	Ann Clery

Produced by Hilton Edwards

CHARACTERS

MICHAEL NEWSOME, *a Clerk of the County Court of Ireland*
MOLLY NOLAN, *a young and comely housemaid*
JAMES STAPLE, *a Sergeant of the Civic Guards*
JULIA O'SULLIVAN, *a housewife*
TEAZIE, *her daughter, a pretty little girl with a lisp*
REDMOND O'HANLON, *a lame Justice of the County Court of Ireland*
★SEÁN O'FENETIC, *a Government Inspector*
DANIEL O'CONNELL, *a Barrister-at-Law*
ARGUS O'HONE, *a Barrister-at-Law*
CRILLY DUFFY, *a Bank Clerk*
MARGARET MARY ALLEN, *a housewife*

The action of the play takes place in the small town of Cloonmore on a snowy day in the present time

★ Pronounced 'Shawn.'

ACT ONE

The study of JUSTICE REDMOND O'HANLON *on a snowy morning in the present time. The study is a gracious Georgian room, untidy and run-down, with shabby Georgian furniture. There is a door at stage right and another door set at an angle on the same side. Between them is a large fireplace with a spacious couch or chaise-longue placed before it. Close by is a cupboard for drinks. Centre back there is a large door which is approached by two shallow steps, and at stage left a large window with a balcony outside. There are several bookcases between windows and doors, and a magpie's nest of rubbish on the tables and chairs. Several classical prints hang on the walls, but most prominent is Botticelli's 'Birth of Venus' which hangs centre back. This is obviously the room of an elderly bachelor.*

[*The Justice's Clerk,* MICHAEL NEWSOME, *comes running in from the door centre back.*]

CLERK: Justice! Justice! Justice! Have you heard the news?
   Put on your topcoat and put on your shoes;
   There's trouble, bad trouble, coming round the bend.
   Justice! Justice! Justice! Can't you comprehend?
   [MOLLY, *a young housemaid, enters at a run from the same door.*]
MOLLY: Oh, Mr Newsome, what is all the fuss?
   It's early, very early to be waking us.
CLERK: Justice! Justice! Justice!
   [*To* MOLLY]: Is he in his room?
MOLLY: You know he never rises till the sun's in bloom.
   [*She opens the door to the bedroom at an angle to the stage, and looks in.*]

CLERK: Justice! Justice! Justice! Can't you hear me call?
[*To* MOLLY]: Wake him in a hurry or they'll sack us all.
MOLLY: He isn't in his bedroom and his bed's a sight.
He must have had a seizure in the night;
There's blood on all the pillows and the sheets are torn.
CLERK: It's urgent that we find him, for I've come to warn
That there's trouble like a cyclone and it's on its way
A phalanx of Inspectors who'll be here to-day.
BOTH: Justice! Justice! Justice!
MOLLY: Are you up or down?
CLERK: Before the sun strikes midday they'll be in the town
Investigating records, Minute Books, and judgement debts,
With microphones and microscopes and fingerprinting sets.
MOLLY: But why should the Justice fear investigation?
CLERK: Because no one welcomes screening in this or any
nation.
Once you get investigators then you get an allegation,
If you get an allegation you appoint ten new inspectors,
The new inspectors find, if they want to keep their station.
They're examining suspicions and anonymous conjectures,
MOLLY: Justice! Justice! Justice! Is he in the bathroom?
CLERK: Justice! Justice! Justice! Is he in the hall?
MOLLY: Justice! Justice! Justice! Is he in the garden?
CLERK: Justice! Justice! Justice! Can't you hear us call?
MOLLY: I think I hear him now and he's in the hall.
CLERK [*opening door to the stairway*]: Oh, Justice, we've been
searching every nook and cranny for you.
MOLLY [*looking over his shoulder*]: My dear man you must be
crazy, sure that's not the boss at all.
[*Enter the* SERGEANT.]
CLERK: Sergeant, have you seen the Justice anywhere?
SERGEANT: I've come to tell the Justice that there's trouble near.
This morning on the phone one of my men
Got word of an Inspector sent to look
At every Station Book and Minute Book.

CLERK: I heard the same from Dublin. He's disappeared.

MOLLY: Why should the Justice resign or disappear?
Only last night he said
That he was the happiest man, awake, in bed,
At table, on the bench. And now he's gone.

CLERK: 'Happy' is a dangerous word in the lexicon
Of youth or age – as ancient writers mention,
Call no man happy who has not earned his pension.

MOLLY: He's careless and gay, that's all you can say;
He'd rather go fishing than waste a fine day
In hearing how lads lead the young girls astray.

CLERK: Or of dangerous driving upon the highway.

SERGEANT: Oh, he's careless and gay, but it isn't hearsay
That his legal decisions alarm and dismay
All those who love law and deplore its decay.

MOLLY: But he's honest and upright and bright as the day.

SERGEANT: Or so we all say.

CLERK: Aged forty, he came thirty years ago
And knew, or so I'm told, some kind of law
Would listen to an argument or two,
Strike out a summons with a legal flaw.

SERGEANT: Then he weighed evidence in equal scales,
Would listen patiently to either side.

CLERK: Then give his judgement in Augustan prose
In which he took a scholar's honest pride.

SERGEANT: He wore two little pins, and one was gold
To show he spoke the language of the Gael,
The other told the world he had renounced
The company and ribaldry of ale.
He would rebuke young girls who flashed their legs
In silk temptation on the witness stand;
The fines imposed on careless publicans
Caused doubt and consternation through the land.

CLERK: *Sed, tempora mutantur*, as you know;
The Justice too has altered with the times,

And he regards as holy virtues now
The weaknesses he once denounced as crimes.
It wasn't very long till he had learned
The world looks better through a glass of malt
Then one by one the Seven Deadly Sins
Took his defences at the first assault;

SERGEANT: Pride in his office grew to Vanity,

CLERK: Soon he was covetous of greater place.

MOLLY: Lust had its day and many a night with him
And Anger etched its pattern on his face;

CLERK: The Glutton's paunch swelled now beneath his gown.

SERGEANT: Envy distilled its bile and made him ill,
Sloth weakened him, slowed down his bloated body
And stultified his intellect and will.

[*There is a thunderous knocking on the hall door.*]

MOLLY: There he is now, he's surely forgotten his key.

SERGEANT: Open the door to our poor refugee.

[MOLLY *goes.*]

CLERK: Who knows what change the opening door may
bring?
You, Sergeant, may be a private from to-morrow,
I may be unemployed, the Justice dead,
And Molly sail a river salt with sorrow;

SERGEANT: Or, perhaps the cards be grouped in a Full House,
I, perhaps, will wear Inspector's silver buttons,
You be established, pensionable, safe,
And Molly be spring-lamb always – never mutton.

[MOLLY *enters and closes the door carefully. She whispers.*]

MOLLY: It's Julia O'Sullivan, trouble again,
She wants to swear an Information
And have her daughter's young man arrested
For some nocturnal aberration.

CLERK: Tell her next week will be ample time for it.

SERGEANT: Tell her there's Court to-day, but there's no
crime for it.

CLERK: Tell her that next Court Day she may swear, if she
    wishes,
  A hole in an iron pot . . .
    [*The door swings open and* JULIA O'SULLIVAN *enters fol-*
    lowed, rather sheepishly, by her daughter, TEAZIE. JULIA
    speaks with great passion.]
JULIA: You sons of witches!
  You lousers! You pack of bowseys! I'll have me rights
  If I have to tear the gizzards and the daylights
  Out of you with me two bare hands.
CLERK: Now, Madam, this is no way to demand
  Your legitimate rights.
JULIA: You collection of frights! I'll give you law!
  Janey, what you'll get from me is a puck in the jaw
  Will rattle your brain-box! Or I'll come behind you
  And give you a rattling good kick where it wouldn't blind you.
SERGEANT [*taking out his notebook*]: Now, Mrs O'Sullivan,
    this kind of language might easily cause
  Conduct detrimental to the due observance of the laws.
JULIA: Look at him in his uniform, like a bus-conductor or
  An unemployed postman! Look-at here, me man-o'-war,
  If you speak to Julia O'Sullivan count the cost!
  I'm a peaceable and decent, respectable woman till I'm
  crossed . . .
SERGEANT: I'm warning you again.
JULIA: But if once I'm roused, it wouldn't give me a second
    thought to pull the coat
  Off of your back and cut your throat.
MOLLY: Now Julia, better go home before the Sergeant gets
    annoyed.
JULIA: And who asked you to put in your tuppenceworth?
    You'd be better employed
  Covering your bosom and not be raising bad thoughts in
  the minds
  Of them that's only too obviously that way inclined.

CLERK: A charming gown that suits Molly very well.

JULIA: Oh, indeed, I know Molly Nolan, seed, breed, and generation,
And no doubt she takes after her mother that was a scandal to the nation.

SERGEANT: A charming, well-bred lady which is more than I . . .

JULIA: A strap she was from the day she first put up her hair,
With her eyes taking liberties and leading the lads to the fair,
And marrying only when any innocent man would swear
She was a married woman for better than half a year.

MOLLY: My mother can show her lines, which is more than some . . .

JULIA: And look at me daughter here, an innocent pet
Wouldn't know a man from a woman if they were undressed.

TEAZIE: Oh, Mazie, you're making me blush again . . .

JULIA: Look at her, poor little Teazie, assaulted and shamed,
Her good name gone and the like of you making game
Of what happened to her under the sheltering cover of night . . .

SERGEANT: It's surely about time you came to your point.

JULIA: And when I come to look for the protection of the Court as is only me right
What do I get only abuse and impudence from them that should know better.
Oh, the first thing in the morning the Minister will have a letter.

SERGEANT: Now, now, now. There's no need to raise a fuss.

JULIA: And maybe those that are high and mighty and grand to-day
Will be begging, homeless and bootless, fireless and castaway.

TEAZIE: Ah, Mazie, come home and don't be making yourself a holy show.

JULIA: Oh, there's me gratitude for rearing you in a babby-
    house when over a year ago
  You should have been put to work like this whipster here,
  Instead of getting music-lessons and talking about your career.
TEAZIE: But Mazie, that was your idea.
JULIA: Now, tell them straight
  What it was Crilly Duffy did in your room last night.
TEAZIE: I couldn't bwing myself to wepeat in public what
    occurred in the pwivacy of my woom.
CLERK: Bag and baggage you must both go – this is the Jus-
    tice's private room.
JULIA: Private or public, isn't it his duty to hear
  All legal complaints? and I'm standing ready to swear
  An Information against Crilly Duffy. Gawney I'll soften
    the cough
  On that fellow before he's very much older – acting the toff
  With his yellow boots and no breakfast, a double-breasted
    waistcoat
  And a hard collar should be cutting his hair-pin of a throat,
  And the accent of him! You'd think he'd cut his lip trying
    to find the way
  Into a porter bottle! Oh, things has changed since my day.
  If a half and half like that tried to give me the beck
  I'd have caught him by the back of the collar and shook him
    till I broke his neck.
TEAZIE: Oh, ma, you're terrible.
SERGEANT: I'm afraid I'll be having to take official cognizance
    of your language.
JULIA: Ah, take a bottle of stout for your breakfast.
  Look at Miss Particular here, thinking herself too grand for
    the local gossoons,
  Has to take up with a Bank Clerk – to go with the piano
    lessons!
  And the next thing he's into her room, like a rat up a down-
    spout;

But I'll put a stop to his gallop, if I have to pull his innards out.

I'll go to the chief local practitioner,

And he'll damn soon bring me to swear an Information before a Peace Commissioner.

Oh, it wasn't to-day or yesterday that Julia O'Sullivan was brought out.

I wasn't reared in a teapot looking out through the spout.

CLERK: I very much doubt that the Justice has jurisdiction so to abridge service.

JULIA: Oh, fiddle me faddle, and keep that kind of chat for the Civil Service, the Lord preserve us!

I'm going down now to the town's best solicitor,

And there's one thing sure, and that's that he's going to be no Conciliator.

TEAZIE: Oh, ma, why must you always bwing the family into diswepute?

JULIA: Another word out of you and I'll give you a clatter on the ear that'll keep you quiet for half a minute.

Come on out of that, you forbidden fruit!

[*She pushes* TEAZIE *in the back and rushes her through the door. There is silence for an appreciable moment. The* SERGEANT *takes off his cap and wipes his forehead — Phew!* MOLLY *drops into a chair. The* CLERK *shakes his head.*]

MOLLY: For fifteen years her husband closed his ears,

And then God pitied him and sealed them up.

SERGEANT: If she succeeds in entering that case,

The Justice must sit, and then the jig is up.

The stupidest Inspector in the world

Would see through his performance.

CLERK: Now war's declared, and now each embassy

Reddens the night with flare of burning papers.

We'd best be heading for the frontier too

Before steel shutters trap us everywhere.

SERGEANT: I'll dump my uniform and burn my baton.

My brother has a fine substantial farm.
My sister has a pub where I can work.
CLERK: Good-bye then, Court and Law, farewell the volumes
  Shoulder to shoulder in leather discipline;
  Farewell the warrants, summonses, decrees,
  I'll think of you when, lounging in a ditch,
  I boil my billycan of tinker stew.
  Farewell authority, dark tie, white collar,
  Farewell umbrella, and goloshes too;
  Head up, I'll march into the last dissolve
  And leave departing footprints in the snow.

  [JUSTICE REDMOND O'HANLON *enters briskly, his head
  swathed in bandages. He has a lame leg, but apart from that
  he is a remarkably well-preserved man of over seventy, though
  he looks about fifty.*]
JUSTICE: Why this meeting in my room?
  You're a very sorry group for a bright and frosty morning.
MOLLY: Where have you been? There's a man on his way
    here . . .
SERGEANT: This morning on the phone one of my men . . .
CLERK: He wants to look at all the books.
JUSTICE: Now, one at a time. What kind of a man?
CLERK: An Inspector who's doing the best he can
  To catch the Justices of this land;
  He examines the books, to check the hand
  That signed against the hand that ordered,
  To see that all fines are recorded.
  To see if the lawyers follow the law
  If Justice is held in sufficient awe,
  Or if Justice and Justices are merely a mock.
  He's arriving, sir, at eleven o'clock.
JUSTICE: Better send him a wire and explain
  That my head has been injured and I am in pain.
  Molly, get me hot coffee as black as tar.
  [MOLLY *goes.*]
I

CLERK: He's on his way, sir; he's in his car, sir
　　I don't advise it, but if I were you sir
　　I'd sit in court at eleven o'clock, sir
　　Or else he might think that it was a mock, sir.
　　The list is light, but still you should sit.
SERGEANT: Your head, sir; how did you injure it?
JUSTICE: Last night, coming through the gate
　　Some villain struck at me with a stick,
　　I parried him, threw him with a judo trick
　　Over my left shoulder, for luck; in the flick
　　Of an eye he was gone. Some lunatic.
　　I've a temperature. My pulse is flying.
　　Newsome, ring the Inspector and say I'm dying.
CLERK: He may be already in the town.
JUSTICE: Then get me out my bands and my gown.
CLERK: Your bands and your gown, sir – you haven't worn
　　　them
　　Since you said that that girl in that case had torn them,
　　The one that threatened the action, sir, for . . .
JUSTICE: Someone must have a gown I can wear.
CLERK: In a town like this, sir? A gown in Cloonmore?
　　The teacher *has* a gown, but he swore
　　The time you fined him he'd have revenge.
JUSTICE: Oh, to-morrow we'll make him ample amends.
　　Even though it's only B.A. –
　　And a pass at that – it will save the day.
　　Now, that's all settled. You'll hide the book.
CLERK: Oh, I couldn't do that, sir. He'll want to look
　　At *all* the books. Justice Slight at Clough
　　Played hide-the-thimble, and, sir, the shock
　　Of what the Inspector did and said.
　　Was such that he hanged himself in the shed.
JUSTICE: Slight hanged!
SERGEANT: And Justice Dill, poor man . . .
JUSTICE: Yes? Yes?

SERGEANT: It isn't known for sure, but they guess
   That the body they found . . .
JUSTICE: My God!
CLERK: The Inspector is very devoted to God
   And the Church. And the Devil too.
   He sees his work in every blot and plot
   And thinks he rules the country towns.
   And I'm very sure he would take it ill
   That people are sworn here on 'Fanny Hill'.
JUSTICE: It doesn't really matter a bit
   If it's 'Tristram Shandy' or Holy Writ,
   The Evangelist John, or Jean-Paul Sartre –
   The truth and the whole truth is what we're after;
   Perjury is perjury still
   On Holy Bible or 'Fanny Hill'.
   But perhaps you'd better go down to the town
   And borrow a testament and a gown.
CLERK: Shall I take your car, sir? The snow is deep.
JUSTICE: My car! God damn your cheek!
CLERK: That's all right, sir. I suppose I can walk,
   But the time is short till eleven o'clock.
JUSTICE: Newsome, my boy, my temper is short
   As my leg. And see that there's heat in the Court.
   Give the Sergeant a lift. Combined we'll up-end
   The Department and all the Inspectors they send.

> [*The* CLERK *and the* SERGEANT *go. The* JUSTICE *stands staring through the window.* MOLLY *enters with a cup which she puts down; she comes to him and holds her face up to be kissed. He backs away from her, horrified.*]

JUSTICE: Now, now. Not in the daylight, and not at the
   window.
   What *would* people think if they looked at us now?
MOLLY: Think, sir? Think about me or you?
   They guess about me. They know about you.
JUSTICE: Know what about me?

MOLLY: My mother said,
   'Don't stay in a room where there is a bed
   And Mr O'Hanlon; like Mary and Kate
   And Brigide and Annie who found out too late
   That Mr O'Hanlon, with one leg in the grave
   Has learned in his Court how men misbehave.'

JUSTICE: What nonsense. Before I was called to the Bar
   I knew . . . that's to say . . . stand back, there's the car.
   You're a very nice little girl, but to-day
   Just behave yourself and keep away,
   As far away as you can from me.
     [*He gives her a quick kiss, pulling himself away with an obvious effort.*]
   Now, no more. Did you bring me that coffee?

MOLLY: It's as strong and black and sweet as . . . as sin!

JUSTICE: Now, none of that. And you must dress up neatly
   Smile demurely, modestly, sweetly,
   Dust the drawing-room, light the fire,
   Tell the Inspector should he enquire
   That you work here only by the day.
     [MOLLY *points through the window.*]

MOLLY: The Sergeant's back with something to say.

JUSTICE: Let him in while I go and dress this scar.
     [MOLLY *leans through the window.*]

MOLLY: Come on up, Sergeant. The door is ajar.

JUSTICE: I suppose I'd better wear a wing-collar;
   It will cut my neck, but impress the Inspector.
   And then, some law-books, and a snuff-box, and even a clean shirt.
   And a phrase or two of Latin to dismay and disconcert:
   In flagrante delicto, Honor virtutis praemium,
   Fiat justicia, even though *ruat coelium!*

MOLLY: It's Irish I'm told all Civil Servants speak.
   Would he understand you if you spoke in Greek?

JUSTICE: I'll go then to prepare a face to meet the faces that
  I meet.
  [*He goes to his bedroom and the* SERGEANT *enters.*]
SERGEANT: I came to tell his nibs the Inspector passed
  Through Clough this morning; the Guards there rang.
  This will be a great and terrible day for every man
  In Cloonmore town.
  [*He takes off his cap, clears off an armchair, and sits on it. He
  draws* MOLLY *to him.*]
SERGEANT: I hadn't a chance to kiss you all the morning.
MOLLY: And if himself came in, what would I do?
SERGEANT: Spit in his eye. He daren't do a thing.
  We both could swear that he was chasing you.
MOLLY: Oh, Sergeant, that old ibex after girls!
SERGEANT: Old step-in-the-hollow thinks of little else.
  [*He kisses her and she sits on his lap, her arms around his
  neck.*]
SERGEANT: Let's talk of love.
  [*There is a noise in the next room and* MOLLY *tries to get up.
  The* SERGEANT *holds her tight.*]
MOLLY: Oh, God, he's coming in.
SERGEANT: And do you think old dot-and-carry is jealous?
MOLLY [*coyly*]: Besides, the morning is no time for love.
SERGEANT: What better time? The little birds are singing,
  The sun is bright as Venus on the snow;
  You're rested, flushed with sleep, your eyes are shining,
  And every ceiling's decked with mistletoe.
MOLLY: But in the morning there is work to do.
  Who can afford to waste time making love?
SERGEANT: Time's made for lovers, and the brightest time
  Is made for love. At night a man is tired,
  But in the morning all his spirit's up,
  His flesh is willing and his tongue inspired.
MOLLY: Waiting for buses and making love I find
  The two great time wasters of mankind.

Love's always good, but I like mine at night.
I don't think love's quite proper in the light.

SERGEANT: We'll compromise. I'll love you in the day,
And you will love me when the sun's away.
A double love will prove a double treasure,
And pleasure doubled is love's greatest treasure.
     [*The door to the* JUSTICE'S *room opens a crack and he peers
     out at them. They hear the door and jump apart.*]

MOLLY: Oh, now we're destroyed. He'll surely sack me now.
Lend me a comb. There's lipstick on your face.

SERGEANT: You're over seventeen and safe to court.
     [*He is scrubbing his face with his handkerchief when the*
     JUSTICE *enters. The bandage is gone and he has a piece of
     elastoplast on his forehead. He pretends to have noticed
     nothing.*]

JUSTICE: Molly, you've surely other work to do.
Blood on your handkerchief, Sergeant? You cut yourself?
You're blushing, Molly! And the Sergeant too!

SERGEANT: The O'Sullivan case, sir. A bit embarrassing –
A man in a girl's room in the dark of night.
I was telling Molly. [*He turns to her.*]
     Now go about your work
I'll tell the Justice all about the fight.
     [MOLLY *goes.*]

JUSTICE: I saw the O'Sullivans go as I came in,
One of them flushed with youth, the one with gin.

SERGEANT: She wants to swear an Information
For malicious damage, burglary, larceny,
Wants the case entered for hearing to-day.

JUSTICE: Yes?

SERGEANT: Mrs O'Sullivan heard a noise last night
At half past ten in little Teazie's room.

JUSTICE [*aside*]: I'd swear it was eleven.
     [*The* SERGEANT *looks shrewdly at him.*]

SERGEANT: The door was bolted but she forced it in

And found young Duffy leaning out the window
Shouting a man had just made his escape.
No one believed him since there is a drop of fifteen feet.

JUSTICE: Nearer twenty I'd say.

SERGEANT: He said he hit the man a savage blow
And wants me to examine all the town.
To find who bears a lacerated head.

[*The* JUSTICE *fingers his forehead.*]

SERGEANT: Julia insists there was no man but Duffy
And Teazie was the only one assaulted.

JUSTICE: Oh, very serious, very serious.
But I never could hear the case to-day.

SERGEANT: I better arrest him,
Caution and charge him in the usual way.

JUSTICE: We can have him up on the next Court day.

SERGEANT: But this is a case of unusual interest.
There might even be points of law involved!

JUSTICE: Law is it? Law? If we followed the law
How many of your cases would ever be solved?
When I was young I studied the law,
I learned my Contracts and Jurisprudence,
But after thirty years on the Bench
I know that such subjects are only for students.
Substantial justice is what I do,
Res ipsa loquitur is the rule I follow;
Each case is tried upon the merits
And legal quibbles I will never swallow.
Now, a case in point – if I found my wife,
And thank the Lord that I haven't got one,
In flagrante delicto, that means Caught in the Act,
Should I question her as to what she had done?
And give her time to invent excuses?
No, I'd take the evidence there before me,
A blushing lover, her lipstick smeared,
And kick the two of them out of the door.

SERGEANT: Well, Justice, at your age to be getting married!
    Congratulations! It goes to show
    That age can't wither a bachelor heart
    And that one leg runs as fast as two.

JUSTICE: What do you mean, I'm getting married?

SERGEANT: Isn't that what you said? And to little Molly!
    And aren't you the daring man to take her!

JUSTICE: Sergeant, is this malice or folly?

SERGEANT: There isn't a lad in all the county
    That hasn't courted Molly some time.
    [*Musingly*]: She'd be just the age to be your grand-
    daughter.
    It's a good thing, sir, that you're in your prime.

JUSTICE: Sergeant, I have no designs on Molly.

SERGEANT: I better tell the neighbours the news.

JUSTICE: Do no such thing. And I'd remind you
    Of the law relating to Slander of Women.

SERGEANT: Well, I'll forget it, if you'll forget
    The *flagrante delicto* and the *res ipsa loquitur*
    And it's nice to know
    That the Justice and Sergeant have something in com-
    mon
    If it's only – a knowledge of the law.
    [MOLLY *shows the* CLERK *in. She wears a fresh frock. The*
    CLERK *has a gown in a bulging brown-paper parcel.*]

CLERK: The teacher wants a guinea a day for the use of his
    gown.
    I said we'd pay.
    [*The* JUSTICE *unfolds the gown which is monstrously ill-
    fitting.*]

JUSTICE: What a sight.
    Chalk and snuff on it. And no bands to wear.
    Molly, get an old collar. I'll make a pair.
    [MOLLY *goes into the bedroom.*]

CLERK: I hear that the Inspector's almost here

Trailing a history of despair and fear,
Clerks, Guards, and Sergeants are being sacked everywhere.

SERGEANT: This case must go on. Burglary, larceny, malicious damage.

CLERK: If you'll come to my office I think we'll manage.

JUSTICE: That case must not be entered to-day.

SERGEANT: That's not what the Inspector is going to say.

[*The* CLERK *and the* SERGEANT *go. The* JUSTICE *drops exhausted into a chair, old and weary.* MOLLY *enters with a soft collar. He immediately pulls himself together and takes the collar.*]

JUSTICE: Now, Molly, observe my sleight of hand.
This was only a collar . . .

[*He tears the collar along the fold to within half an inch of the end.*]

JUSTICE: . . . and now it is bands.
Get some elastic, stitch it on here, discreetly,
Cut off the button-hole, finish it neatly.
Now when the Inspector arrives, if he's young,
Don't stand as if someone had bitten your tongue;
Be nice to the gentleman, and if he should wish
To be pleasant – well, what's in a kiss?
And if he is old, stand near; that's no crime,
The way you stood close to me the first time.

MOLLY: What's in it for me?

JUSTICE: If you are good, I'll not tell your mother
A word of the Sergeant, a word of the others.

MOLLY: My mother indeed! I've no secrets from her.
It's you and not me should be fearing my mother!

JUSTICE: I fear your mother, my Molly, my sweet!
I knew your mother when she was neat
And lovely as you, with the same black eyes,
The geranium lips to hypnotize;
But that was twenty-five years ago
And your mother to-day goes slack and slow

As you will too. To look at you now
Who could believe it? Flawless brow,
Eyebrows like brackets, the little hand
That will harden and coarsen and wrinkle like sand,
The waist that's half the span of an arm,
The shape that leads young fellows to harm –
And old fellows too – will broaden and thicken,
The blue white of your eye will yellow and sicken,
And you will forget, as your mother forgets
And wonder why you have only regrets.
For that is the history of girls everywhere,
The wild and the sweet who'll make love in a chair,
Once they get to the age of the double-bed
Become respectable matrons instead;
While a man, though he's only a leg and a half,
Will remember all his adventures and laugh
To think that though old and a little grey
It isn't quite time yet to kneel and pray
And repent the nights when he was gay.

MOLLY: God bless us, Justice, if you were young
You'd destroy the girls with your flattering tongue.

JUSTICE: When I was young I had no need of flattery
And no one charged me with assault and battery;
But now my honey words must soothe and soften
The armed resistance that I meet too often.

[*The* SERGEANT *enters and looks through the window.*]

SERGEANT: Here he is now in a little car.
He's stopped. He's getting out, looks at the sky
Takes out a rolled umbrella. What a face,
Pale, cold, and shapeless as a licked ice-cream.

[*There is a knock at the door and the* CLERK *enters.*]

CLERK: The servant of the people is without;
He has an electronic brain,
His eyes are hard and bright as paper-clips,
His blood is office-ink, red-tape his veins.

JUSTICE: Then let us face him. Clear the room for fight.
  Stow rags and rubbish under every chair.
  You, Newsome, speak in Irish to him,
  That language princely, comely, noble, fair.
    [*The* CLERK *goes and* MOLLY *and the* JUSTICE *work
    rapidly to set the room to rights.*]
JUSTICE: We'll straighten pictures, dust and disinfect,
  Open a book here – 'Archbold on Criminal Law',
  Cover that shameful crack with modest curtain
  So forge our picture, fair without a flaw.
  The curtain rises on the saintly Justice,
  Philosopher and friend, jurist and scholar,
  The kindly smile, the wise, distinguished face,
  The head on hand above the starched wing-collar,
  The brow's fine parchment wrinkled a thought with care,
  The hand draped gracefully upon the knee.
  Enter a villain now to kettledrum.
    [*To* MOLLY]: Molly, show in the man immediately.
      [*The room changes its character and becomes respectable.*
      MOLLY *goes and the* JUSTICE *adopts the pose he has de-
      scribed. After a moment the* INSPECTOR *is shown in. He
      carries a brief-case and an umbrella. The* JUSTICE *stands up
      and clasps him warmly by the hand.*]
*[INSPECTOR: *An Breitheamh Redmond Ó hAnnluain?*
JUSTICE: And who may I have the pleasure . . .?
INSPECTOR: Seán Ó Fenetic from the Department. A little
  inspection.
JUSTICE: Ah yes.
INSPECTOR: *Tá athas mór orm casadh ort, a Bhreithimh.*
JUSTICE: Oh, *tá, tá,* I mean *seadh, seadh:*
  My Irish is gone with my Algebra,
  But there was a time when I wore the ring
  With *An t-Athair Peadar* and *An Craoibhinn Aoibhin.*]
INSPECTOR: Justice O'Hanlon, I am honoured to meet you.

  * Non Irish-speakers may omit the passage in square brackets.

JUSTICE: The honour is mine, I'm very sure.
   Would you like a cup of coffee or tea –
MOLLY: Or better still, a glass of good whiskey?
   [*The* INSPECTOR *fingers his total-abstinence pin.*]
INSPECTOR: Whiskey's a beverage I have never drunk
   And judging by its influence on others
   I'm never likely to fall into that error.
   Coffee I find is over-stimulating;
   So, if you'd be so kind, a cup of tea.
   No milk or sugar lest I should take pleasure.
JUSTICE [*to* MOLLY]: Whiskey was a most improper thought.
   A pot of frightened tea for the Inspector.
INSPECTOR: Frightened tea! Indeed, that's very witty,
   And you'll find, Justice, I'll appreciate
   All kinds of wit and humour in the country.
   I'm always noted for my sense of fun!
JUSTICE: Oh, you'll find wit and humour in Cloonmore.
   I scarcely think you'll find our Court a bore.
INSPECTOR: Cloonmore – bore, Oh, that's extremely good!
   I must remember it. To-day's Court Day
   I'm glad to see. I'll sit beside you, Justice,
   On the Bench and see how Justice is done.
   This, I must tell you, is a purely informal inspection.
   There's been, you know, some talk of laxity,
   Not here of course, but in some other Counties,
   But I am glad to say the law still rules.
JUSTICE: *Fiat justicia ruat coelum.* Unhappily to-day we have
      no cases,
   So you must hear me grant some licences
   For petrol, dancing, drinking on Fair Days.
INSPECTOR: How shocking! People dance still in Cloon-
      more?
   And drink on Market Days?
JUSTICE: In moderation. I heard that Justice Dill . . .
INSPECTOR: An excellent and conscientious man.

JUSTICE: Had disappeared.

INSPECTOR: He reappeared.

JUSTICE: And that poor Justice Slight had hanged himself.

INSPECTOR: He had, it's true, an accident with a rope;
But he is quite recovered and I found
Nothing to censure, except a slight addiction
To poker and intoxicating liquor.
He'll be retiring shortly but will have
A little crick in the neck for the rest of his life.

[*He gives a roar of false laughter, and demonstrates the crick.*]

INSPECTOR: Ah yes, we find that after thirty years
Some of your colleagues, very few, it's true,
Have quite forgotten all the law they knew;
They have abandoned the Rules of Evidence.
Preferring to decide by common sense.
And so they are retiring one by one.

JUSTICE: They must be all as old as a bush by now.

INSPECTOR: Ah, now you mention it. I meant to ask
About your own age. You'd now be . . .

JUSTICE [*brazenly*]: Fifty-nine.

INSPECTOR: You must have been a very young appointment.

JUSTICE: A stripling.

INSPECTOR: We've never seen your Birth Certificate.

JUSTICE: Burned in the Custom House long years ago.

INSPECTOR: Ah yes, indeed. And when our man went down
To find your christening date – the page was gone.

JUSTICE: How very strange. In what years did he look?

INSPECTOR: He might have been mistaken. It was 1888.

JUSTICE: But that would make me over seventy years.
Who could remove that vital piece of evidence?

INSPECTOR: The adversary is powerful, I've seen his work
As I have visited the country towns;
I realize the Devil may have withered
That missing page. The Devil is very powerful.
But powerful also is the Civil Service.

Some day we'll surely find that missing page.
JUSTICE: You might as well seek the Philosopher's Stone,
    Or lost Atlantis, the missing bone
Which Adam exchanged to buy him a wife.
It will never again be seen in this life.
INSPECTOR: How can you be so certain?
JUSTICE: Because I know that village – the most evil
    Little village, where the Devil
Stalks in daylight with his daughter by his side,
And every year he takes a village bride.
Now, if your man had examined any year,
No matter which, the Devil still would tear
That page out. Had he looked at '94
He'd find that page in ashes on the floor.
INSPECTOR: You say the Devil is active there?
JUSTICE: Active? He's adolescent!
    So that at times no one can be certain
If it's reality they see and hear,
If it's their wives who join them in their laughter
Or if in the dark they hold the Devil's daughter.
She is so beautiful that one half glimpse
Can set most saintly men to breeding imps.
INSPECTOR: But surely, Justice, you exaggerate?
JUSTICE: The grace of the Devil's dark and luscious daughter
    Can come between the eyelid and the eye
When you're at prayer. The Sainted Anthony
Knew no temptation that she can't supply.
Burnish your rosary with eager fingers,
Add to your scapulars, hang holy pictures
On every wall till they are thick as grass
And still the Devil fills each room with music.
Oh, I could tell you stories, but I won't,
Lest you should think that I – exaggerate.
INSPECTOR: My man was lucky to come back alive.
JUSTICE: But in Cloonmore the angel hordes

That guard it from the evil of the world
Are visible in daylight to the pure
And in the darkness shine for the profane.
Ah! This is Ireland's very navel, here
No foreign newspaper distorts the Sabbath,
No poteen drives men mad or women wild
And public houses close their doors at ten
(In winter; half past ten in summer.)
I cannot claim that this is all my work,
The people are a simple, honest race
Unspoiled and truthful, and it well may be
That any Justice would have done as well.
To-day, as you have mentioned, is Court Day
And yet, apart from certain licences
There is as I have said no work to do.
The Court can be adjourned and you will come
And see our model town before we lunch.

INSPECTOR: All that you say amazes me. I'm glad
That one small town has shed the Devil's power,
But sad I cannot see you doing justice.

JUSTICE: I am an old, old man believing first
In ancient virtues and the power of truth,
The integrity in the heart, the even scales,
Held in a steady hand, convinced that right
Will always conquer error, and the rule of law . . .

[*The door bursts open and* JULIA *rushes in, pulling* TEAZIE
behind her.]

JULIA: So that's where you're hiding yourself, you step-in-
the-hollow, you fright,
And your clerk letting on you'd taken leg-bail and hopped
it to Dublin or London in the dead of the night.
Oh, I have you now, and there'll be no more shilly-shally-
ing
But I'll swear out an Information if I have to go to the
Taoiseach himself about your dilly-dallying.

INSPECTOR: Justice, who is this extraordinary person?

JULIA: No person at all, but Julia O'Sullivan, that knows her
 seed, breed, and generation.

 And who might you be with the black monkey-jacket and
 the britches like railway tracks coming into a station?

INSPECTOR: Madam, I am an Inspector from the Department.

JULIA: Then you're the bucko I've been waiting to see, for
 the lousers down here

 Won't enter me case for hearing to-day though I'm standing here ready to swear

 That Crilly Duffy was at you-know-what last night in me
 daughter Teasie's room,

 And broke a valuable vawse in addition to trying to turn
 himself into a bridegroom.

JUSTICE: Mrs O'Sullivan, this is the first I have heard of your
 case

 And it is very inconvenient to hear it to-day of all days,

 But if it is urgent it will, of course, be heard

 Since speedy justice is the letter of the law, and the word.

INSPECTOR: Justice, I'm charmed to hear that after all

 I'll see a justice who loves law and right

 Adjudicate. I'll join you at the Court.

 Excuse me while I go and tell my driver.

 [*Exit.*]

JULIA: If that mealy-mouthed ruffian is expecting to get an
 earful he will,

 For the story I've to tell has more fire and poison in it than
 a poteen still

 And before the day is out the town of Cloonmore is going
 to hear its fill.

JUSTICE: Since there's no help for it, let's light the powder-
 mill.

CURTAIN

ACT TWO

SCENE ONE

The Courthouse at Cloonmore. On the stage level are a large table for the use of counsel or solicitors, and several chairs. On stage left is the witness-box, stage right, benches for witnesses. On the next level is a bench for the CLERK, *and above that another bench for the* JUSTICE *and the* INSPECTOR. *The harp of Ireland is displayed on a plaque above this bench and green, draught-proof curtains hang at right angles on either side.*

> [*On the rise of the curtain the* JUSTICE *is on the ground level in gown and home-made bands; he carries a very old grey-brown wig. He is talking to* TEAZIE.]

JUSTICE: You must learn to lie if you're a woman,
   Must look me in the eye and tell your lie,
   Dimple a little, as if you're half uncertain,
   Then gently tell your lie.
TEAZIE: I've told enough already to be damned.
JUSTICE: What lies?
TEAZIE: That Crilly was the only man last night came to my
   room.
JUSTICE: No lie that. He was the only man.
TEAZIE: And you?
JUSTICE: I am a Justice. So that was no lie.
TEAZIE: I said that no one jumped out of the window.
JUSTICE: No lie there. I fell after your young man nearly
   split my skull.
TEAZIE: I said I kissed no man last night.
JUSTICE: Quite true. You kissed no man,
   But I, sweet child, kissed you.

When you are questioned you will tell again
How Mr Duffy, driven half insane
By jealousy and most impure desire
Came to your room unasked and then imagined
A demon lover beautiful as fire.

TEAZIE: But that was you.

JUSTICE: Mention no names save Lucifer and Bael and
    Behemoth.

TEAZIE: I'll not remember those.

JUSTICE [*slowly and impressively*]: Lucifer and Bael and
    Behemoth;
    And don't forget that one incautious word
    May ruin you and Mr Duffy both.

TEAZIE: The evidence you promised?

JUSTICE: All in good time. Embezzlement's no joke
    And if the bank should know that Crilly Duffy
    Had swindled them for twenty thousand pounds
    They'd be annoyed.

TEAZIE: But what you promised was
    That if I let you in last night you'd give,
    Exchanging it for one chaste kiss of mine,
    The evidence. Where is the evidence?

JUSTICE: These things are never simple, and to-night
    If you will leave your door and your hall-door
    Unlatched I'll come again and I'll explain.

TEAZIE: My ma is awful mad.

JUSTICE: Mothers with lovely daughters need to be
    Philosophers or else insane, and few
    Have intellect to read philosophy,
    So they are mad. Your evidence to-day
    Is simple. You were standing at your door
    Alone. You went into your room, alone, and, still alone,
    Heard someone battering at your door. You opened
    And there was Duffy, screaming wild abuse,
    Accusing you of infamy and he

Grabbed a great weapon and attempted murder.
All his imagination. No one was there
Except yourself enchanted in the moonlight.

TEAZIE: But didn't he nearly crack your skull in two?

JUSTICE: Now, don't confuse the issue. I have told
All that you need to know. If you are good
This morning and to-night your wedding-present
Will be the evidence against that lout.
Promise.

[*He is about to kiss her when the door opens and the* INSPEC-
TOR *enters in gown and bands, very neat and clean by com-
parison with the* JUSTICE. *He carries a shining white wig.
The* JUSTICE *backs away from* TEAZIE.]

JUSTICE: Promise that never again you'll try to speak
To me of any case before the hearing.

INSPECTOR: Quite right. And this young lady?

JUSTICE: Miss O'Sullivan. She came to plead
For her fiancé who is charged to-day
With multifarious criminal activities.

INSPECTOR [*to* TEAZIE]: No doubt your motives were most
praiseworthy,
But as the Justice says no Justice may
Discuss a case which is *sub judice*.

JUSTICE: Go now.

TEAZIE: And don't forget the evidence you promised.
[*She goes.*]

INSPECTOR: What did she mean?

JUSTICE: Who knows? To simple people law is a mystery.
[*The* INSPECTOR *adjusts his wig.*]

INSPECTOR: And now for facts. It's time that we begin.

JUSTICE: On to the fray and may the best man win.
[*They mount to the bench by steps at right. At the same time
the* CLERK *enters and mounts to his bench by steps at left.*
O'HONE *and* O'CONNELL, *two barristers enter, and sit at
counsels' table. The* SERGEANT *stands beside the witness box.*

JULIA, TEAZIE, CRILLY, *and* MARGARET MARY ALLEN
sit on the witness benches, CRILLY *apart.*]

CLERK: I now declare this Court open.

JUSTICE: Gentlemen, this is a glorious day,
For me, for you, for all here in Cloonmore,
For sitting on the bench for all to see
Is this fine man, a Government Inspector.
His name is Seán O'Fenetic, come to explore
This little paradise at Heaven's door.
I welcome him, as you must welcome him,
Regretting that he never came before.

INSPECTOR: It is indeed a pleasure to reply
To such whole-hearted generosity
Such as in all my journey till to-day
I had not met. Your Justice has told me of
This happy, happy spot, where virtue glows
As bright as wallflowers in a cottage garden,
Where . . .

[JULIA *hauls herself to her feet and goes towards the witness-box.*]

JULIA: Shut your gab and get on with the work,
Do you think I've me day to waste. I'll soon knock the
smirk
Off of your lardy face.

SERGEANT [*moving towards her*]: That's enough now, Julia.

INSPECTOR: The Justice will be forced to commit you for
contempt.

JULIA: Contempt is it? Contempt! Oh, young man don't tempt
Me vocabulary.

JUSTICE: Sergeant, take her into custody till the rising of the
Court.

JULIA: Oh, don't gaol me. I'll swallow me patience like castor
oil and let you have your sport.

JUSTICE: No. No. Take her into custody immediately and
we will adjourn her case.
This is the most fortunate contempt of all my days.

INSPECTOR: Fortunate?

JUSTICE: Unfortunate, of course.

JULIA: I'll rake the backyard of me mind for good little
    words like Prunes and Prisms,

  And I'll promise you on me benders to use no more Anglo-
    Saxonisms.

INSPECTOR: Perhaps she is sincere, and she is after all an
    amusing example of rural oddity.

JULIA: You lousy . . . [*She swallows.*] Prunes and prisms.
  [DANIEL O'CONNELL *rises to his feet.*]

O'CONNELL: I appear for the plaintiff if your Honour pleases.

JUSTICE [*to* INSPECTOR]: Mr Daniel O'Connell.

O'HONE: And I appear, if it please your Honour, for the
    Defendant.

JUSTICE: Mr Argus O'Hone.

O'HONE: I would apply for an adjournment to the next Court.
  [*He exhibits one small sheet of paper.*]

  My instructions are incomplete and the notice short.

JUSTICE: A very reasonable request. Adjourn to the next
    Court.

INSPECTOR: My time in Cloonmore is also short.

  I am certain the Justice will give every consideration

  To the fact that the defence is embarrassed in a case of this sort.

JUSTICE: Very well then, Proceed.

CLERK: Are the parties ready in O'Sullivan and Duffy?

JULIA: Let me at that box and I'll soon show you.

  [*She goes to the witness box.*]

CLERK: Take the book. Say these words after me:

  'I swear by Almighty God that my evidence in this case
    shall be the truth, the whole truth and nothing but the
    truth.'

  [JULIA *repeats the oath after him.*]

JUSTICE: You may sit down.

JULIA: And do you own the flippin' seat? [*Effort.*]

  I mean, thank you very much. [*She sits.*]

O'CONNELL: Now, your name is Julia O'Sullivan?

JULIA: Sure don't you know that as well as I do.

O'CONNELL: Yes, is enough.

JULIA: All right, but when are we coming to what Crilly Duffy did in my daughter Teazie's room last night?

O'CONNELL: All in good time. Now Mrs O'Sullivan you live I think at the Shambles end of the town and you have a daughter by name Teresa?

JULIA: Teresa she was christened, and the priest said that a lovelier name there wasn't in the calendar of the saints. Oh, if he could see her now with her short skirt hooshed up on a bicycle and her face all covered with paint. Not but she's a good girl, or was till last night. And her hair tossed and her lipstick smudged. Oh, Janey, there was the sight!

O'CONNELL: You have, we gather, a daughter by name Teresa.

JULIA: Teazie we call her, and her father often said 'Teazie be name and Teazie be nature.' [*She points*]: There she is, bold as brass and her face all red.

[TEAZIE *hides her face in her hands.*]

O'CONNELL: Well, we seem to be advancing. Do you recall the events of last night?

JULIA: Look at here Mr O'Connell, you know damned well that I remember last night. Wasn't it I told you what happened and came here to kick up Hell's delight!

O'HONE: She seems to be succeeding admirably, if I may say so, your Honours.

O'CONNELL: Perhaps you would tell us in your own words what occurred last night.

JULIA: And whose words have I only me own? I heard a noise up in Teazie's room and says I to meself . . .

O'CONNELL: What did you do? Don't mind what you said.

JULIA: That's trouble, says I to meself, ran upstairs and found the door barred in me face. Let me in, says I, or be the

hokey – because from the noise inside I knew there was
some kind of jiggery-pokery . . .

INSPECTOR: A strange phrase. [*To* O'CONNELL]: Perhaps
you could construe?

JULIA: The words of it!

O'HONE: Perhaps I could assist your Honour. Jiggery would
suggest to me the sound of a dance measure, as in Jig, while
pokery I take to refer to the atmosphere of mystery as in a
'pig in a poke'.

O'CONNELL: My friend has been too gently reared. The jig
which my client had in mind was a dance measure indeed,
but not that of the dance-floor. And pokery – well, I refer
your Honour to Freud and folklore.

INSPECTOR [*writing*]: Most enlightening. I have always been
most interested in country matters.

O'CONNELL [*to* JULIA]: You decided to investigate?

JULIA: Let me in quick, says I, getting into a state. Ma, says
she, I'm fast asleep and good-night. But I looked through
the keyhole and there was me brave Crilly Duffy standing
full of fight. So I burst me way in, and there was the sight.

O'CONNELL: Well now, describe to the Court what you saw.

JULIA: What do you think I'm doing? There was the mattress
and the wire knocked off the bed. St Joseph broken and St
Patrick left for dead, the hand basin and the ewer and me
mother's decorated pot were smashed and scattered like
petals on a garden plot. I gave Crilly a clock on the dial that
made him rock.

JUSTICE: No doubt there will be a cross-action for assault, so
let us adjourn

And hear all the cases together, preferably next term.

O'HONE: My client realizes that appearances are against him,
and is prepared to waive his rights.

JUSTICE [*disappointed*]: Oh.

JULIA: I'll have the law on you, says I, coming into the room
of me innocent pet, says I,

I'll have you charged, says I, before the Courts, says I,
And sent to gaol, says I, for asssault, says I,
Don't you fret, says I.
Oh, will you, says he, and what did I do, says he,
But the same as you, says he.
If you'd seen, says he, what went on between, says he,
This wan, says he, and a class of man, says he.
What class of a man, says I. Oh, a shocking looking villain,
    says he,
But I gave him a stroke, says he, and his skull must be
    broke, says he,
For he was hot, says he, with, saving your presence, the pot,
    says he,
And that's why it's broke, says he. That's how he spoke.

JUSTICE [*puts his hand to his head and winces*]: That blow was
    no joke.

INSPECTOR [*automatically*]: Says he. Oh, excuse me.

O'CONNELL: And is that all you can tell us?

JULIA: All is it? I've a catalogue of complaints as long as to-
    day and to-morrow,
And a bill for the ewer and basin and the bedclothes I had
    to borrow,
And me pain and suffering and poor little Teazie's charac-
    ter gone,
Not to speak of the *sine qua non*.

O'CONNELL: The *what?*

INSPECTOR: The *what?*

JULIA: Me mother's pot with the roses like an old sweet song
    all done be hand
That used to be as bright as Christmas in its little house in
    the wash-hand-stand.

O'CONNELL: And how would you estimate the damage?

JULIA: Fifty pounds I say for the lot, neither more nor less,
And that's including me own labour free for cleaning up
    the mess.

O'CONNELL: Thanks, Mrs O'Sullivan.

JULIA: For nothing.

[O'HONE *rises to cross-examine.*]

O'HONE: Now Mrs O'Sullivan, I want to go back on your evidence.

JULIA: Go back on it is it, and every word as true as Brian Boru.

O'HONE: Let us recapitulate.

JUSTICE: He means he wants to start all over again.

JULIA [*coyly*]: There's a man for you!

O'HONE: Please, Mrs O'Sullivan, let us eschew unseemly levity.

O'CONNELL: My friend should know that lawyers' true felicity
Is found alone when wit is wed to brevity.

O'HONE: *Touché.* Now Mrs O'Sullivan, you are not, I think, a native of Cloonmore?

JULIA: A native is it? I'm a native of nowhere, but a decent Dublin woman that was shanghied down here
Among a lot of hungry mohawks and savages, with their stirabout faces and pigs' ears.

O'HONE: Quite. And Mr Duffy is also of Dublin origin?

JULIA: Oh, Dublin I grant you, but not my Dublin at all.

O'HONE: And you must also be aware that his mother is a woman of considerable wealth and influence with the bank?

JULIA: So that explains his swank.

O'HONE: And you knew that he was due to a transfer back to Dublin, and thought that if you could blackmail him into marrying your daughter you could go with them.

JULIA: Oh, there's a thing to say about Julia O'Sullivan.
Oh, there's libel and slander.
I wouldn't have that half-boiled monkey married to me daughter if he was rich as Alexander.

O'HONE: And you knew perfectly well that there was another

man in the room, but are willing to cloak it because if you admitted it there would be no marriage.

[JULIA *jumps from the box and makes for the door.*]

JULIA: Well, my answer is N.O. – No, to anything you ask or suggest. And I'm answering no more questions.

TEAZIE: Ah ma, come home. What'll daddy say when he reads it in the paper?

CRILLY [*rising to his feet*]: I say, on a point of order. May I ask a question.

JUSTICE: Certainly not. You are represented by counsel.

CRILLY: It's only just, you know, the question about the paper. I mean couldn't all this be hushed up. Though I'm as innocent as you are I'd be willing to pay up and shut up . . .

JUSTICE: Good man yourself. Case settled. Decree for the full amount with costs.

O'CONNELL: Most satisfactory.

INSPECTOR: If the Defendant has a defence it should be heard in full, since some might swear that full justice was not done. The case must go on.

CRILLY: And can we keep the whole thing out of the papers?

JUSTICE: Sit down at once, sir, or you will join the plaintiff in a cell.

CRILLY: Oh, not that, sir. That would be exchanging Purgatory for Hell.

JUSTICE: The Plaintiff refusing to be further cross-examined, her case fails and I will strike it out.

INSPECTOR: Two solutions occur to me. Either Mrs O'Sullivan might conduct her case herself, which she is indubitably capable of doing, or Mr O'Connell, in spite of the irregularity might continue as her counsel while we keep in mind the contempt that has taken place.

O'CONNELL: I suppose I had better. I call Miss Teresa O'Sullivan.

[TEAZIE *is called to the box and sworn.*]

O'CONNELL: Now tell us in your own words what happened last night.

TEAZIE: He rushed into my room and said there was somebody there. But no one was there but Lucy and Bill and Bizmuth.

O'CONNELL: Who are these people? Local friends? Though Bizmuth is a most exotic name.

TEAZIE: I was alone, but he wouldn't believe me, so I invented Lucy and Bill and Bizmuth.

O'CONNELL: And then?

TEAZIE: Oh, he was wild and he said that I was evil,
And if there wasn't a villain in the room it surely was the devil.

INSPECTOR: Ah! [He writes.]

TEAZIE: He used foul language and threw the furniture around a lot,
And out of the window went my mother's pot. Then she came up and she told you the rest.

O'CONNELL: Thank you, Miss O'Sullivan.

O'HONE: Now, first of all, Miss, who told you of these devils?

TEAZIE: I made them up.

O'HONE: Could they in fact be LUCIFER and BAEL and BEHEMOTH?

TEAZIE: Something like that.

INSPECTOR: Three of the greatest enemies of mankind,
Once splendid angels of the Seraphim.
Child, where did you learn the chorus to this Satanic hymn?

JUSTICE: Preaching last Sunday our good Parish Priest
Spoke of these very demons and they stuck
Like wasps in jam in this child's simple mind.

O'HONE: You tell us then that for a simple 'No'
You set three rampant demons in a row?

TEAZIE: Well, I was told . . .

O'HONE: Don't mind what you were told. Just answer Yes or No.

TEAZIE: I was that confused I didn't know what to do.

O'HONE: I must suggest that your whole story
Is far from fact as truth from history.

TEAZIE: I'm a good little girl and I've always been good,
When other girls went to the bog or the wood
When fellows were whistling and other girls giggling,
When fellows were squeezing or whispering or tickling,
While other girls sported in meadow or sand
I was home in my room with my beads in my hand.

O'HONE: As you were last night in evil company.
  [*He hums to himself, beating time with his pencil.*]
  Tick, tack, toe, my mother had a . . .

INSPECTOR: What is the meaning of this?

O'HONE: The song of the cobbler, as the witness should know.
  I'm suggesting, you see, that Larry, the local cobbler, was
    the man in the room.
    [*He points dramatically at* TEAZIE'S *feet.*]
  Where did you get those shoes, miss?

JUSTICE [*sotto voce nods and whispers to* TEAZIE]: Larry.

TEAZIE: Larry.

O'HONE: Delivered when?

TEAZIE [*looks towards* JUSTICE, *who mouths* 'Last night']: Last
  night.

O'HONE: And it was he who was in your room?

JUSTICE: No doubt he brought the shoes, and then to see
  Whether they fitted went up quietly,
  Was frightened by the noise that Duffy made,
  Jumped from the window and left you there afraid.

TEAZIE: That's how it happened.
    [*The* SERGEANT *comes over and whispers to* O'HONE.]

O'HONE [*delighted, rubbing it in*]: I see. That's how it happened.

TEAZIE: Innocent he came, innocent went.

O'HONE: Innocent he came, innocent went!
  Aren't you the little lying innocent.

JUSTICE: Mr O'Hone.

O'HONE: Aren't you the smooth-tongued, practised little liar,
    Conjuring rampant devils from Hellfire,
    Incriminating innocent shoemakers,
    And turning bankclerks into skilled heartbreakers!
        [TEAZIE *begins to cry.*]
    Answer me, miss. Tears are not evidence.

INSPECTOR: Mr O'Hone, on this question of evidence, per-
    haps you can assist me?

O'HONE: Gladly, your Honour.

INSPECTOR: You first suggested to the witness that there was
    a cobbler in her room last night.

O'HONE: Yes, sir.

INSPECTOR: When she accepted that you turned on her and
    said the shoemaker was innocent.

O'HONE: For a very good reason, since I've just been in-
    formed that the cobbler left for Dublin yesterday and won't
    return until some time to-night. [*He turns to* TEAZIE]: Miss
    O'Sullivan you've in fact admitted someone was in your
    room last night. Who was it?

TEAZIE: With all the questions I've grown addle-witted.

O'HONE: I must demand an answer.

TEAZIE: I was told that if I said . . .

O'HONE: Don't mind what you were told. Answer my ques-
    tion. Who was in your room?

TEAZIE: It was the . . .

JUSTICE: I notice by my watch that it is one o'clock,
    Time for the lunch recess. No doubt the shock
    Of all these questions is too much for the witness.
    She will be calmer after the recess.

O'HONE: But I must demand an answer to my question.
    She was about to give that vital answer.

JUSTICE: That's what I . . . hoped.

O'HONE: Had not your Honour suddenly interloped.

JUSTICE [*urbanely*]: Not I, but Time. Time, that's the friend
    and enemy

Of man. Time that will set us free
Of Time *in* Time; Time that will bring us back
To this same Courtroom in an hour, unpack
Its treasures and reveal the truth.
Time's an Inspector with a weasel's tooth.

CLERK: This Court stands adjourned until two o'clock. All stand.

> [*There is a black-out to indicate the passage of an hour. In the darkness a clock strikes two.*]

SCENE TWO

One hour later. The Court has reassembled, but JULIA *and* TEAZIE *are missing.*

CLERK: O'Sullivan v. Duffy at hearing. Are all the parties here?

O'HONE: I had not concluded my cross-examination of Miss O'Sullivan.

CLERK: Miss Teresa O'Sullivan.

SERGEANT: No answer from the witness.

O'HONE: This is disgraceful. She was about to tell
What man was in her room. And now she's missing.

JUSTICE: Further contempt of Court. Plaintiff refused to answer questions,
Now she and all her witnesses have gone.
The case is finally dismissed with costs.

MARGARET MARY: I'm here, your Honour, and not disappeared.

JUSTICE: You're here! And who are you when you're at home?

MARGARET MARY: Home or abroad I'm Margaret Mary Allen,
Here as a witness to what went on last night.

JUSTICE: I have dismissed the case.

O'CONNELL: With very great respect,
I have established a *prima facie* case
Of rowdy conduct and malicious damage.
I'm calling Mrs Allen, though what she'll say
I can't imagine.
[MARGARET MARY *goes to the box and is sworn.*]

O'CONNELL: What have you to say?

MARGARET MARY: Last night when the moon was shining silver white
I took my telescope and saw a sight.

O'CONNELL: Your telescope?

MARGARET MARY: My husband was a lightship man for
    years,
When he retired that was his souvenir.

O'CONNELL: What did you see?

MARGARET MARY: What I had hoped and what I feared to
    see:
A villainous old man's debauchery.

INSPECTOR: Could you see his face.

MARGARET MARY: The eyes had almost left my startled head,
When I saw this villain sitting on the bed,
But though my hand was trembling I could see
That he was old and marked with villainy.

JUSTICE: Your piety has not improved your looks.

MARGARET MARY: This horrible old lecher was sitting on the
    bed,
His arms held out to Teazie as if he said . . .

O'HONE: Comment.

MARGARET MARY: Come to me, learn how to be bad!
The door swung open; in came the other lad.

O'CONNELL: What other lad?

MARGARET MARY: The light was bad; I couldn't rightly see.
The bad old girl-trap ran straight for the window,
The other took a thing from down below
And hit him as he jumped into the snow;
Then the old fellow threw something in his face . . .

CRILLY: Snow mixed with gravel.

MARGARET MARY: And that held up the race.
He ran across the garden leaving traces,
Very queer traces that looked like demon's paces.

INSPECTOR: Ah! Demon's! [He writes.]

MARGARET MARY: I went down later and I followed them.

O'CONNELL: Where did they lead?

MARGARET MARY [pointing to the JUSTICE]:
To that man's house.

SERGEANT [*softly*]: That's done it.

MARGARET MARY: Straight up the path and vanished at the door.

JUSTICE: At my door? [*He laughs.*]

MARGARET MARY: I had a vision.

JUSTICE: Visions now!

MARGARET MARY: A vision of yourself and Behemoth
  Drinking a flaming bowl of witch's broth.

JUSTICE: Was it in Technicolor? [*Sycophantic laughter.*]

O'CONNELL: You said these footprints led to the Justice's house.
  And then what more?

MARGARET MARY: No more. But I felt the beat of leather wings.
  [O'CONNELL *sits down and* O'HONE *rises.*]

O'HONE: No studies in demonology for me. But facts.
  Your telescope?

MARGARET MARY: What do you mean, *my* telescope?

O'HONE: Is it just possible that the sergeant here
  Might charge you with receiving stolen property?

MARGARET MARY [*lamely*]: It was a souvenir.

O'HONE: What other souvenirs have you at home?
  Are you prepared to stand a thorough search?
  [*There is no answer.*]

O'HONE: No answer. The Court will know what weight to place
  On the evidence of such a witness. I have no further questions.
  [*She leaves the box.*]

JUSTICE: Mr O'Hone? Do you wish to go into evidence?

O'HONE: May it please your Honours.
  This case, as has been said, is very strange,
  A simple case of damage to a pot,
  Some furniture awry, a slight assault
  Is now confused with demonology.

K

Perhaps my client can explain. Christopher Duffy.
> [CRILLY *comes to the box and is sworn.*]

O'HONE: Now tell us briefly what occurred last night.

CRILLY: I saw her talking to a man outside;
They went upstairs, the door was open wide.
'Twenty thousand pounds,' I heard him say,
She said, 'Where's the evidence?' I couldn't stay
Longer in hiding there so I ran in
And found this old man tempting her to sin.

O'HONE: What old man?

CRILLY: I couldn't see. The light you see was dim.
I was so raging that I took the pot
And hit him, or, as the plaintiff said, I hot
Him on the head. He jumped through the window,
Bent down and blinded me with stones and snow.

O'HONE: Now tell us of your relations with this girl.

CRILLY: I am a gentleman. I must not speak.
I'm sorry for the questions that were asked.

O'HONE: I have no further questions so.
> [O'CONNELL *rises.*]

O'CONNELL: You broke the valuable pot?

CRILLY: Under extreme provocation.

O'CONNELL: Don't mind the provocation. Damage was done?

CRILLY: Yes, and I'm only sorry I didn't see his face.
> [JULIA *rushes into Court, followed by* TEAZIE.]

JULIA: Maybe you didn't see it then, but you see it here,
And look at it well with its dirty old monster's leer.
I'm sorry young man that the ruffian you gave the clock
Is where he is instead of being in the dock.

JUSTICE: Sergeant, arrest this woman instantly.

SERGEANT: I'm very sorry, your Honour, but I have an urgent appointment elsewhere;
I'll come back later, if I have time to spare.
> [*Exit.*]

JUSTICE: Sergeant, return at once. Your superiors will hear
    about this.

SERGEANT [*at the door*]: That's the very thing I'm afraid of.

JULIA: Oh, so you're losing your army.

O'CONNELL: Mrs O'Sullivan, you really must control your-
    self.

JULIA: Control meself. That's all I've heard all day
    But I'm here now and I'm going to have my say,
    And if anyone tries to stop me I'll raise such a stink
    That it isn't only Jembo who'll be out of a job as quick as
    a wink.

INSPECTOR: Mrs O'Sullivan, your case is closed.

JULIA: Ah, don't give me any of your ould Civil Service
    double-talk;
    I didn't come down in the last shower – think I'm a Hawk!

INSPECTOR: I don't understand you, but what have you to
    say?

JULIA: Will I tell you in me own words?
    [*speaking very fast*]: Well, then, in me own words:
    When I got home I found this daisy was missing,
    And I caught her at the station with the engine just hissing,
    Oh, I gave her dog's abuse, but she said, 'Ma, honest, I
    didn't do a thing,
    But if I told the truth I'd never see a wedding-ring.'
    'How's that?' says I, so she told me about this scoundrel
    Letting on Crilly had swindled the bank for twenty
    thousand pounds,
    And luring himself into her room be the promise of giving
    her evidence.
    And then Crilly came in and caught him on the job
    And he said that if she told on him he'd tell how Crilly, the
    slob,
    Was caught by him with the twenty thousand pounds . . .

INSPECTOR: Please, Mrs O'Sullivan, oh, please, stop for a
    moment.

Who is this man you have called 'scoundrel', 'Jembo',
'Him', and other vague expressions?

JULIA [*laughing hysterically*]: Who is your man? Who is your
jills? You must be dead and blind

Sure anyone in his senses would know who that was . . .
[*She breaks down, laughing and sobbing.*]

JUSTICE: A short adjournment while Mrs O'Sullivan re-
covers from her gin.

[*To* CLERK]: Let's get away before the roof falls in.

CLERK: This Court stands adjourned.

[*The* JUSTICE *takes the* INSPECTOR *firmly by the arm and
leads him from the bench.*]

JULIA [*recovering*]: Who is the greatest oul' ram and rascal
since Moses was in the Highlanders!

[*She looks at the Bench.*] They're gone! But I'll catch them if
I have to travel to Dublin on my benders.

MARGARET MARY: Come now, Mrs O'Sullivan, and say a
little prayer;

It will calm you down, and so will the fresh air.

JULIA: Prayer is all right, but at home I've a blackthorn stick
That'll beat salvation into that heretic.

Come on the whole lot of you till I beat him sore and sick.

CURTAIN

ACT THREE

The same as Act One. A few minutes after the close of Act Two.

[*The* SERGEANT *enters. He is very distraught, his cap is off and his collar unbuttoned. He is followed by* MOLLY.]

SERGEANT: With these two hands I could choke that meddle-
some old trot.
MOLLY: What's happened now?
SERGEANT: The case was nearly over when in she landed,
Margaret Mary Allen, if you please,
And now she's landed us all in the same cart.
She told the Inspector what we all suspected.
I'm running out. You'll come too if you're smart.
MOLLY: Where to?
SERGEANT: What does it matter. We'll run away to
safety.
MOLLY: I'm safe enough.
SERGEANT: Then run away to love.
MOLLY: But where? And why?
[*He puts his arm around her waist.*]
SERGEANT: Any road can be love's avenue.
What's wrong with buying us a caravan –
I've cash enough for that – then we'll roll south;
No uniform, no stripes; authority
Abandoned. We'll rise up in the dawn
Make love before the light has chilled our eyes
Gather our breakfast from a farmer's yard.
Then down the road in the pink light of day
With air as light and warm as a first kiss.
MOLLY: And then?
[*He sits with her on his knee.*]

SERGEANT: Oh, we'll find ways to live. We'll deal in horses,
    Sing an old ballad, tip the winning horses.

MOLLY: And have a Sergeant always on our track.

SERGEANT: We'll fear no Sergeant, but Sergeant Death himself,
    And only in old songs have lovers died.

MOLLY: You're the romantic Sergeant!

SERGEANT: Too long the law and I have been allied
    And she's a bleak-faced, cold, and bloodless wife;
    No heady, beddy girl of twenty years.
    Now I've grown young again in face of danger
    That pumps adrenalin into my veins.

MOLLY: Then you're too young for me. What I can see
    Is not the waking in the nursery glow
    Of film coloured dawn, but rain for breakfast
    And for supper rain, an appetite
    Unsatisfied and healthy all day long.

SERGEANT: I'll get a steady job then, and buy you dainties
    To bring to you for lunch. Then we'll make love.
    [*She pushes away his hands and rises.*]

MOLLY: That's all you old men ever think of – love!

SERGEANT [*shocked*]: Old!

MOLLY: You must be thirty-five if you're a day.

SERGEANT: That's not old!

MOLLY: Old. Old and tired. You only *talk* of love.
    If you were young you'd not be sitting there.

SERGEANT: I'm on the run.

MOLLY: Well run then.

SERGEANT: And I am young and vigorous as any poet
    Ever alleged he was in lying rhymes,
    And when I was a Guard went to the Bishop
    Because of what I told the Parish Priest.

MOLLY: When you were a Guard – A Guard and young!

SERGEANT: Now I'm a Sergeant, sure I'm twice as bad.

MOLLY: I'll not come with you so. Respectability is what a
    girl is needing at my age.

I've been a wild girl, some allege I'm bad,
But when I marry it will be a lad
Respectable and wealthy, one who is
As new to love as the first schoolboy's kiss.
And the first kiss that he will get from me
Will be when we are wed respectably.

SERGEANT: God bless us, Molly, where is there such a man?

MOLLY: And he'll respect me, as you never could
Who have some memories of field and wood
Where I was foolish once – that very place
In our first row, I'd get it in the face.

SERGEANT: I'd promise never . . .

MOLLY: I know you'd try . . .

SERGEANT: Never to say a word of Murphy's barn . . .

MOLLY: You see, it's there.

SERGEANT: Or mention haystacks, ditches, fields as white
And starred with daisies as a summer's night.

MOLLY: They'd all be with us from morning to nightfall,
Like sainted pictures on an old maid's wall.

SERGEANT: So then I must be going on my own?

MOLLY: Why go at all?

SERGEANT: There'll be a fearsome scandal, everyone
Connected with this case will bathe in trouble.
Good-bye Molly, give me the last, sweet kiss.

[*He kisses her. There is the sound of knocking downstairs, then* JULIA *is heard shouting, 'It's open.'*]

SERGEANT: Here's that old hairpin. Hide me out of sight.

[MOLLY *pushes him into the* JUSTICE'S *bedroom.* JULIA *rushes in followed by* MARGARET MARY. *She carries a large stick.*]

JULIA: Where are the heroes till I lather them with my stick,
Beat them sore and sorry, good-looking and sick.

MOLLY: Who are you looking for?

JULIA: You know damn well – the so-called Justice and that
mealy-mouthed serpent

That took my little pet's good name and he pretending to
  be a Civil Servant.

I'll Civil Servant him, so I will, himself and his wig and
  gown,

And I'll get the people together and run him tarred and
  feathered out of the town.

MARGARET MARY: Mrs O'Sullivan, what would Father Martin say?

JULIA: Father Martin can mind his own interference for this
  one day.

  [*To* MOLLY]: Where is he, I'm asking? Trot him out here
  quick.

  Or I'll leave you all a heap of ruins with the aid of my
  blackthorn stick.

MARGARET MARY: Oh, Mrs O'Sullivan, come down to the
  church I say.

JULIA: *Laborare est orare* – to belabour is to pray.

  And I'll belabour those two buckos. Come on now, where
  are they? [*She shakes* MOLLY.]

MOLLY: The Inspector's gone off in the train, and the Justice
  with him.

JULIA: The train doesn't go for a good ten minutes.
  Come on till I hit them.

  [*She rushes out followed by* MARGARET MARY.]

SERGEANT [*emerging from the room*]: She'll do murder yet, but
  if it's only the Inspector

I'll stand behind her and make the law her protector.

MOLLY: Don't be stupid, sure the Inspector won't be at the
  train.

SERGEANT: True for you.

  [*Loud footsteps are heard downstairs.*]
  Who's that now?

MOLLY: Get back in the room. [*He goes. There is a knock at the
  door.*] Come in.

  [*The* CLERK *enters, half intoxicated.*]

CLERK: My bag is packed. Two tickets on the plane.
  We'll get away before we're sacked or slain.

MOLLY: Who'll get away?

CLERK: You'll come with me. We'll marry and be glad.

MOLLY [*sotto voce*]: Are you my wealthy and respectable
  lad?

CLERK: Eh?

MOLLY: How old are you?

CLERK: I'm thirty-two.

MOLLY: Your salary?

CLERK: It was a poor six hundred. In Australia we'll be as rich
  as Guinness.

MOLLY: Not so young. But guileless and respectable.
  He'll do. Have you ever kissed a girl?

CLERK: Only in dreams. I've too much fear of Hell.

MOLLY: The Inspector seems to think that this is Hell.

CLERK: If this indeed were Hell and you the Devil
  I'd come to you though I should swim through evil.

MOLLY: But you know very well that I'm no Devil.

CLERK: If angels love in Heaven as we on earth
  You then have been an angel since your birth;
  If greater angels have the greater love
  Then you are greatest in the place above.

MOLLY [*aside*]: This is a schoolboy's dream of virtuous
  love.

CLERK: But if Cloonmore should need a patron saint
  O be its patron, I will make my plaint;
  Sweet saint, perform a miracle and be
  Sweet to no one on earth, save only me.

MOLLY [*aside*]: This must be drink and drunk virility.

CLERK: But if it's true that in the pearly Heaven
  No human love is asked, and none is given.
  Then let us build our human Heaven bright
  Against the winter and the fall of night.

MOLLY [*aside*]: He must have lost his senses with the fright.

CLERK: Hell is your absence, Heaven where you are;
   I am the navigator, you the star.
MOLLY [*aside*]: He must have learned this eloquence in a bar.
CLERK: I think, when I hear talk of love and kisses –
   Here is a sober-sided one that misses
   Love's light libido, all life's lovely links
   In the last lousy dribs and drabs of lawyer's ink
   If I must have a drab, let it be Molly,
   I told myself, and ran here full of folly;
   But now I look at you and see you are
   No drab or slattern, but my evening star.
MOLLY: And *did* you learn this love-talk in a bar?
CLERK: At Heaven's golden bar, where you smile down.
MOLLY: You learnt this poetry in Cloonmore town?
CLERK: No, but in books that once were only books,
   But now are gardens ripening in your looks.
MOLLY: Why all this sudden love and poetry?
      [*The* SERGEANT *enters.*]
SERGEANT: I saw him in a pub a half-hour since;
   That was the golden bar where he learned eloquence.
CLERK [*jealously*]: What are you doing here?
SERGEANT: The same as you, trying my luck with Molly.
   What set you drinking, you that had the pin
   Since old God's time?
CLERK: If drinking is a sin, what's perjury and perversion of
   The golden mean of justice? Besides I'm cold.
SERGEANT: A ball or two of malt and you'd abduct
   The only lissom girl in Cloonmore town.
   Shame on you!
CLERK [*abashed*]: Marriage is what I offered.
MOLLY: No less would be accepted.
SERGEANT: I have the first refusal.
MOLLY: You've had it. Now, if you're going, go.
CLERK: Someone is coming.
MOLLY: Hide then, the two of you.

[*They both go into the bedroom. The* JUSTICE *enters, very dispirited.*]

MOLLY: I hear that Mrs Allen talked too much.

JUSTICE: When the ship's scuttled all talk's too much.
   I better pack my bag.
   [*He goes towards his bedroom.*]

MOLLY: I'll pack it for you. Best sit down and rest.

JUSTICE: All life will be a rest from this day out,
   If I can get away.

MOLLY: Where are you going?

JUSTICE: Where the first boat is bound.
   [MOLLY *goes into the bedroom.*]

JUSTICE: I've always wished a celebrated case
   To make my name, spread my distinguished face
   Across the vulgar news-sheets; when I win it
   The case is celebrated – but I'm in it.
   I've always wished to leave a famous name
   At which both learned and vulgar would exclaim:
   'Whatever law was lacking, he could add it!'
   I've had my wish. In fact I'd say I've had it.
   Yes, I have had it, I who sat above
   The badger-pit of squalid hate and love,
   Where prurience can always conquer prudence
   But for the overruling Jurisprudence,
   Where greed and envy, sloth and lechery
   Are matched with perjury and treachery
   And only the cool, remote judicial brain
   Keeps anarchy from winning the campaign.
   Now I am in it because my ageing blood
   Sought the desirable before the good,
   Because lust conquered law and falsehood truth –
   For though my body is Age my heart is Youth. . . .
   [TEAZIE *enters very softly.*]

TEAZIE [*whispers*]: She didn't get you so?

JUSTICE [*startled*]: No. Who?

TEAZIE: My mazie's out with a blackthorn stick
  And she swears if she catches you or the Inspector
  She'll leave you a heap of ruins.
JUSTICE: Why did you tell her our little secret?
TEAZIE: What could I do but tell?
JUSTICE: Tell no one that again.
  No one would marry you if they suspected
  That you invited me to your room last night.
TEAZIE: I didn't invite you.
JUSTICE: Now, don't get confused again.
TEAZIE: And anyway me and Crilly are getting married in
      the spring,
  And everything will be right and go like a wedding-ring;
  And he is innocent and didn't steal a thing.
JUSTICE: Like a wedding-bell is what you mean. And nothing
      is right.
  The Inspector will make his report and I'll be sacked before
      the night.
TEAZIE: But now I'm getting married my mazie will surely
      drop the case.
JUSTICE: The case doesn't matter. What matters is the chase;
  And I'd better be off now or go to gaol for all my days.
  And all for a kiss I never even got.
  Come to my arms my innocent cocotte.
TEAZIE: Oh I couldn't. What would Crilly say?
JUSTICE: The first and last before I go away.
TEAZIE: What good is a kiss when that is all you'll get?
JUSTICE: There speaks philosophy. Why open wine that you
  will never drink?
TEAZIE: Eh?
JUSTICE: Oh, come with me wherever I may run.
TEAZIE: But even if I wanted I'm too young;
  'Gaol bait' my mother calls me.
JUSTICE: 'Although my body is Age my heart is Youth.'
TEAZIE: I'd rather stick to Crilly, that's the truth.

JUSTICE: Who would not rather be a youthful crook
 Than an old judge who must love by the book.
  [*He catches her around the waist. She disengages herself.*]
TEAZIE: But I thought you said . . .
JUSTICE: Don't mind what I said, just do what I do.
  [*She runs, the* JUSTICE *after her, too slow on his lame leg.
  She runs through the door and on to the stairs. The* JUSTICE
  sits down, panting, MOLLY *enters.*]
MOLLY [*alarmed*]: Are you going to have a stroke?
JUSTICE: I'm going to have nothing as far as I can see,
 No job, no kiss, no future. I will be
 A Maugham old man, a bum on a South Sea pittance
 Combing the beach and waiting a remittance.
MOLLY: No. No.
JUSTICE: Yes. I'm a broken man, an old man now.
MOLLY: Why did you do it?
JUSTICE: What?
MOLLY: Everything. Go up to Teazie's room,
 Tell her of Lucy and Bill and Biz . . .
  [*She breaks down laughing.*]
JUSTICE: All for love.
MOLLY: Love?
JUSTICE: The tragedy of old age is being young,
 An old man knows what's lost; Hell, we are told,
 Is not all Faustus flame, it is the loss,
 The deprivation, the divorce from good;
 And that's old age – the ignorant eye of youth
 Damns by neglect the youthful, amorous heart.
MOLLY: And you have that?
JUSTICE: More than your Sergeant, more than all your
 men.
MOLLY: But Teazie's eye is as blank as death with ignorance.
JUSTICE: Since when have girls been chosen for their brains?
 She has the body of an Aphrodite.
MOLLY: And brains would go to her head!

JUSTICE: Oh, Molly, why do I have to go!
  With you I could be happy. Your daring eye
  Strips the old body off and sees the youth.
  Come with me and we'll marry and be young.

MOLLY: Three offers in a day!

JUSTICE: Who are the others?

MOLLY: Both known to you.

JUSTICE: I have no time for games. You'll marry me?

MOLLY: No.

JUSTICE: Why not?

MOLLY: Too old, too poor, too tired to outstrip the law.

JUSTICE: Not old except in years; and not so poor.
  With you I'd fly to where the sun makes pictures
  All black and white, like the piano keys.

MOLLY: I said before to-day I'd only marry
  A simple young man who is new to love
  And has no memories to reproach me with.

JUSTICE: I have so many memories I'll forget
  Whether your name is Molly, May, or Liz
  And in which century I loved you first.

MOLLY: I'm almost tempted. [*She looks through the window.*]
  What is it worth to you
  To exorcise the Inspector like a ghost?

JUSTICE: What do you mean?

MOLLY: To wake to-morrow as though to-day had never
  been.

JUSTICE: Explain.

MOLLY [*urgently*]: No. What is it worth?

JUSTICE: How will you go about it? And what do you want?

MOLLY [*impatiently*]: I have no time for games. Will you
  make a will
  Leaving me heir to all you die possessed of?

JUSTICE: Why should I?

MOLLY: Ask me no questions if you want to be saved.
  Will you promise?

JUSTICE: I don't understand it, but I promise.
  If you can bring back yesterday's certainty
  I'll leave you all I have.
MOLLY: Swear. [*She takes a testament.*]
  Swear now. I swear that I will make a will
  Leaving to Molly Nolan all I own.
JUSTICE: I swear that I will make a *valid* will
  Leaving to Molly Nolan all I own.
MOLLY: Give me the key to the liquor cupboard.
JUSTICE: Why?
MOLLY [*imperious*]: Give me the key. [*He does so.*]
  Now go into that room.
  And whatever you hear be silent as a chair.
    [*She takes out a brandy bottle and two glasses. He goes into
    the second room.* MOLLY *examines herself in the mirror, wipes
    her lips clean of lipstick. There is a knock, she calls 'Come in'
    and the* INSPECTOR *enters.*]
INSPECTOR: The Justice has not returned?
MOLLY: No. Is the Court adjourned?
INSPECTOR: It is.
MOLLY: What happened?
INSPECTOR: The case is still *sub judice* and cannot be discussed.
MOLLY: Of course, but I could tell you things about Julia
  O'Sullivan.
INSPECTOR [*severely*]: It cannot be discussed.
MOLLY: And as for Margaret Mary Allen . . .
INSPECTOR: A pious lady of undoubted virtue!
MOLLY: But I could tell you things.
INSPECTOR: I'll hear the evidence and trust my judgement,
  Though never has my judgement been so strained.
MOLLY: You must be tired. Sit down. Would you like tea?
INSPECTOR: Yes, I am tired. But no tea, thanks. It is too
  stimulating.
    [*She pulls the couch round before the fire, and switches on a
    table-lamp. He sits.*]

MOLLY: A cigarette?

INSPECTOR: For me no devil's weed
Clouding the heavens with the stench of Hell.

MOLLY: I tried one once and turned green, white, and yellow,
Like the old flag of Erin.

INSPECTOR: We must resist temptation.

MOLLY: Oh, I know,
From secret smoking what evil evils follow!
Boys and girls together, hidden in meadow grass,
Sharing one butt . . .

INSPECTOR: Unhygienic.

MOLLY: But worse. From sharing sinful smoke
Soon they are sharing kisses, kisses lead
As all men know to sin, and those who break
Any commandment soon smash up the ten.
One kiss may make an addict. Kissing is
Habit forming.

INSPECTOR: You have been kissed?

MOLLY [*shocked*]: Inspector!

INSPECTOR: I'm sorry, but you speak with such authority.

MOLLY: One hears these things.

INSPECTOR: One does of course, and I have heard them too,
But would not mention them to innocent girls.

MOLLY [*adoring*]: No. You are strong and good, with truthful eyes.

INSPECTOR: I never learned to lie.

MOLLY: I know. I know. Oh, and that masterful forehead.
Give me your hand.
    [*She sits beside him.*]

INSPECTOR: Why?

MOLLY: I can read palms.

INSPECTOR: A frivolous and possibly sinful pastime.

MOLLY: I learned it from an old and pious nun
A lay-sister as saintly as . . . as . . . yourself.

INSPECTOR: Oh, I don't aspire to saintliness, merely to good.

[*It has begun gradually to grow dark. He holds out his hand.
She peers at it with evident admiration.*]

MOLLY: Oh, what a hand! A map to Eden's country
Before the Devil taught men how to think.
Here is the head-line, like the Euphrates,
The life-line, broad and straight, an Amazon,
The heart-line . . . no, I won't say it.

INSPECTOR: What?

MOLLY: Here is the Mount of Venus . . . no I can't tell you.

INSPECTOR: Can't tell me what?

MOLLY [*putting his hand away*]: No, it's a frivolous pastime.
You were right.

INSPECTOR: No. Tell me.

MOLLY [*taking his hand with feigned reluctance*]:
A good head here for business, and a good heart,
Good judgement, too, clear thinking, charity.
You had some illness in your youth and some
Years of adversity before you got this job.

INSPECTOR: Remarkable. It's all so right. But what of the
heartline?
And the Mount of Venus?

MOLLY: Better not think of Venus, naked slut,
Tempting poor men whose passions are too strong.
Good business instinct.

INSPECTOR: You said that before.

MOLLY: So I did. Success shines like the sun
Naked at midday in an August sky.
That's nearly all.

INSPECTOR: Why don't you tell the rest?

MOLLY: For the same reason that you wouldn't talk
Of cases heard in Court to innocent girls.

INSPECTOR: But I'm not an innocent girl.

MOLLY: I am, and blush
Too easily at the love-story here.

INSPECTOR: Love story?

MOLLY: No let's forget it. I'd better go [*she puts out the lamp*]
  About my work. The light is gone.

INSPECTOR: No. Tell me what you see.

MOLLY: What would the Justice say
  If he came in and found us sitting so,
  Your hand in mine in the romantic gloom.
  [*The only light now is the strong red glow of the fire.*]

INSPECTOR: Put on the light then.

MOLLY: The bulb has gone, I think.

INSPECTOR: You need no light to tell what you have seen.

MOLLY: Then, since it's dark enough to mask my blushes,
  I'll stain my innocence by telling you.
  You see this Mount of Venus, as plump and rounded as
  . . . as . . .

INSPECTOR: As what?

MOLLY: As Venus herself in that naughty picture there.
  See how she rises naked from the sea
  With everything she has on view, God help us.

INSPECTOR: I can't see it.

MOLLY: That is as well. The Mount of Venus shows
  Your love of women.

INSPECTOR: But I've avoided women like . . . like cigarettes.

MOLLY: A good thing too, Inspector, with that hand
  No woman could resist you.

INSPECTOR: Tell me more.

MOLLY: The Mount of Venus is only the beginning.
  The heartline leads from that and shows poor hearts
    bleeding and weeping from indifference.

INSPECTOR: That can't be true.

MOLLY: I only know what's here,
  And if what's here is true you've broken hearts
  In every Department of the Civil Service.

INSPECTOR: And never knew it.

MOLLY: And never knew it. Here
  I see girls entering convents for your sake

Working among black skins for Heaven's sake
And yours; and some that pined and died away
Because they were denied a smile, a word;
And others who have married think themselves
Into your arms each time that they are loved.

INSPECTOR: This is shocking.

MOLLY: It's not your fault, but Nature's
In giving you this irresistible
This magic fascination. . . .

INSPECTOR: Fascination! This is the devil's work.

MOLLY: No, but God's, since you are God's creation.

INSPECTOR: How profound. Perhaps I was intended
To be a great preacher who would rescue women
Through this dangerous fascination you have seen.
Perhaps you have shown me my true vocation?

MOLLY [alarmed]: Oh no, not that. I see no priesthood here,
But women praying for a kindly word.

INSPECTOR: But women are temptation.

MOLLY: To you. To them
You are temptation. Thank God for his night
That masks my blushes while I say such things.

INSPECTOR: I'm blushing too.

MOLLY [putting her hand to his face]: As hot as the watchman's
fire.

INSPECTOR: Molly. . . . Your name is Molly?

MOLLY: Yes.

INSPECTOR: What a lovely name.

MOLLY: The way you say it it's as beautiful
As Aphrodite or Helen, or even Venus itself.

INSPECTOR: All pagans.

MOLLY: Or Deirdre – oh! she was a pagan too.

INSPECTOR: Molly, you have disturbed me.

MOLLY: I didn't want to tell.

INSPECTOR: You have disturbed me deeply.

MOLLY: It's only nonsense really. Forget it all.

INSPECTOR: How can I ever look a woman in the face
   And not be thinking, 'Is this a broken heart?
   Is this girl near to madness for my sake?'
   The responsibility will break me.

MOLLY: You can get a second opinion.

INSPECTOR: No. No. I believe you. I'll have to hide indoors.
   Get a manservant. But what about my job?

MOLLY: Women are sensitive, they feel vibrations
   Through a brick wall, and so you'll break their hearts
   Their little sensitive hearts, not knowing it.
   I pity you, Inspector.

INSPECTOR: And you, yourself?

MOLLY: I myself, what?

INSPECTOR: I mean, do you feel . . . anything?

MOLLY: I've work to do, I must be going down.

   [*She tries to draw her hand away, but he holds on to it.*]

INSPECTOR: Do you?

MOLLY: Do I what?

INSPECTOR: Do you feel this . . . this . . . irresistible fascination?

MOLLY: I'm only an ignorant girl whose feelings
   Are conditioned partly by environment and partly
   By heredity, so my reactions are
   Not typical.

   [*There is a smothered laugh from the next room.*]

INSPECTOR: What's that?

MOLLY: I heard nothing.

INSPECTOR: It sounded like a snigger or a cough.

MOLLY: Someone in the street. I must be going.

INSPECTOR: No. You've raised up this demon, you must
   lay it.

MOLLY: I've only told you what you must have known.
   Surely you've dreamt at night of lovely women
   Holding you in their arms, their perfumed hair
   A veil between your eyes and the shameless light?

INSPECTOR: Sin. Temptation. I've resisted it.

MOLLY: Or in the morning thought of girls as lissom
As free as flame or wave or wandering air.

INSPECTOR: But a cold shower soon skelped them to their lair.

MOLLY: No, for they come again. These are the girls
Who dream at night of you. You are their dream
As they are yours.

INSPECTOR: Those radiant creatures dream . . . ?

MOLLY: Of you. St Paul
Must be your confessor now and set you right.

INSPECTOR: A little wine for thy stomach's sake is what he said.

MOLLY: That too. And he was wise. A drink, Inspector?

INSPECTOR: I've never tasted liquor.

MOLLY: Think of St Paul.

INSPECTOR: He was a Protestant I've always thought.

[MOLLY *pours two drinks. She hands him a glass.*]

MOLLY: Here's to St Paul.

INSPECTOR: My pledge is smashed at last. [*He drinks.*]
My Lord, that's hot. What kind of wine is that?

MOLLY: Cognac they call it, and it's good for chills.

INSPECTOR: Smash one commandment, they say, the rest
will follow.
Because you read my hand I'm drinking wine;
What worse may follow this fiery anodyne?

MOLLY: What did St Paul say?

INSPECTOR: I thought I told you.

MOLLY: No. Something else.

INSPECTOR [*jumps to his feet*]: Not that. Not eunuch for the
love of God.
'Some are born eunuchs, some are made eunuchs, and some
have made themselves eunuchs for the love of God.'

MOLLY: For the love of God sit down. Now try again.
It's there subconsciously, hidden under layers
Of bureaucratic fat.

[*The* INSPECTOR *sits down with a plop.*]

INSPECTOR: Of course. Now I remember the alternatives
   Equally hateful to the Irish male.
   Better, he said, to marry than to burn.

MOLLY: That's it at last.

INSPECTOR: Who'd burn could he escape it? But who'd
   marry
   Were burning not thrown in th'other scale?
   No, I'll take orders and go save the blacks.

MOLLY: Think of those passionate women in whose blood
   The sun runs thick with yeasty vitamins;
   You'd have no peace from them, soutane or no.

INSPECTOR: If I'm to be a walking occasion of sin
   Where is salvation? My thoughts are sinful now
   As any Sunday morning English paper.

MOLLY: Think of St Paul.

INSPECTOR: But I have met no girls. Who'd marry me?

MOLLY: Once you are safely married your temptation,
   That awful double temptation will be drugged
   And you can walk again like other men
   Spreading no evil thoughts like sin's confetti.

INSPECTOR: But I'm too shy. How can I meet a girl?
   What would I say? How would I propose?

MOLLY: But you're not shy with me.

INSPECTOR: That's true enough.

MOLLY: And you could easily propose to me.

INSPECTOR [alarmed]: What's that you're saying?

MOLLY: Oh, nothing.
   [She pours two more drinks.]

MOLLY: Here's to emancipation.

INSPECTOR: Here's to O'Connell, though I'd rather drink
   To Father Matthew, enemy of drink.

MOLLY: What do you earn a year?

INSPECTOR: I've eighteen hundred.

MOLLY: And pay away a third in bachelor's tax.

INSPECTOR: That's very true.

MOLLY [*muses*]: Eighteen hundred. Not bad.
My daddy left a farm, and I'm the heir,
A snug, well-settled farm that pays its way.
INSPECTOR: Why do you work here then?
MOLLY: Rustic boredom.
INSPECTOR: You speak well.
MOLLY: Thank you, my lord. I read a lot.
INSPECTOR: This cognac is strange wine. My head is
light.
MOLLY: Then lay it lightly here.
[*She makes to draw his head to her bosom. He draws horrified
away. She draws him gently back and speaks very softly,
almost hypnotically.*]
MOLLY: No, lay it gently here, don't be afraid.
Fear is the enemy of every joy.
Sleep now a little sleep. My little man,
My lost small boy, what are you running from?
Why do you hide from life inside a cave
Of office files? Life is here, as warm
And generous as your own mother's bosom.
Sleep here. Be easy. Rest. Here is the safest place
In all God's world for you. The simple things
Of life, as simple as your own four bones
That grew with you since your last moment here,
Are here again. Here you have never left
Though you have run and hidden, taught yourself
That what you wanted most was worst, not best.
Here is the end of every setting out,
The harbour where all ships return
And drop their anchor.
[*She enfolds him with her arms, and his arms gradually,
almost somnambulistically surround her.*]
This you must learn again,
To kiss, to bite as gently as a calf,
Caresses softer than a kitten's fur.

And little words as subtle as little spiders,
The whispered words that keep the night awake.

INSPECTOR: Oh, Molly.

MOLLY: What is your name?

INSPECTOR: Seán. But my mother calls me Johnny.

MOLLY: Gently Johnny, my jingle O. Outside
In the bleak world of paper you'll be Seán,
But where the world is soft you're always Johnny.

INSPECTOR: Why have I been afraid?

MOLLY: Fear is a word and we'll have no more words.

INSPECTOR: Easy, you said, if I proposed to you.

MOLLY: Another word. We've no more need of words.

INSPECTOR: And yet I'll say it. Will you marry me?

MOLLY: You are the fourth to-day who asked me that.

INSPECTOR: I'd have been first if I had known you first.

MOLLY: You don't know me at all. A girl in the dark
Who said soft things to you. I'm sorry now.

INSPECTOR: Why sorry?

MOLLY: A thousand reasons that you'll never know.

INSPECTOR: And will you marry me?

MOLLY: An ignorant country girl?

INSPECTOR: I don't care. You're all the girls who tempted
My waking, sleeping thoughts. I've loved you always.

MOLLY: You'll not be sorry. I took one man in my arms
And find another coming alive in them.

INSPECTOR: And so you'll marry me?

MOLLY: I will on one condition, that we leave
Cloonmore to-night and never return again.

INSPECTOR: The unfinished case?

MOLLY: That foolish case. Forget it.

INSPECTOR: Perhaps it is not so foolish, suspicion now
Points its red finger here.

MOLLY: Here?

INSPECTOR: The pious Mrs Allen told of steps
That led from where the fracas was to here

And disappeared. It may have been the devil
But I would like a better explanation
Much as I fear the devil.

MOLLY: Fear nothing more
Devil or man or saint, come to my arms
And dream the other half of my dream:
[*He takes her in his arms and kisses her. There is a long silence.
The two doors to the left open softly and figures can be dimly
seen entering. Suddenly the stage is flooded with hard, un-
romantic light. The* JUSTICE, CLERK, *and* SERGEANT *are
discovered. The* INSPECTOR *and* MOLLY *jump guiltily apart
and sit side by side on the sofa.*]

JUSTICE [*softly and portentously*]: And what is this, Inspector?

INSPECTOR: What is what?

JUSTICE: This un-Irish abuse of hospitality.

INSPECTOR: Nothing has been abused.

JUSTICE: You are invited in friendship to my house
And here I find you in *flagrante delicto*
With my young serving-maid. Shame on you, sir.
And drinking too.

SERGEANT: Perhaps the young lady would like to lay a
charge
Of assault within the meaning of the Act?

CLERK: And I who offered her all I possessed
Am left bereft.

JUSTICE: No doubt the Department will wish to have a
report
Of its Inspector's conduct in the country.
Newsome, prepare it.

CLERK: Instanter, sir.

JUSTICE: That country innocence should be assailed
By sophisticated vice, that the pure mind
Should be seduced by the sleek city sinner!
O *tempora*. To think that I, protector
Of the ancient moral code should find you thus!

INSPECTOR: I only . . .

JUSTICE: *Res ipsa loquitur* – the facts speak for themselves
　　And now, sir, get your hat and get you gone.
　　　[*The* INSPECTOR *rises sheepishly to go.* MOLLY *rises too,
　　　imperiously.*]

MOLLY: No. He'll not go and he'll not be abused.
　　He's my fiancé now. We're leaving town.

JUSTICE: This is strange news, surely untrue, Inspector.
　　While Molly is a charming little girl,
　　I know that sometimes she exaggerates.

INSPECTOR: Incredible. Since the happy rising of the Court
　　I've found my first, last, greatest love.

JUSTICE: Molly, my dear, forgive me. I'm delighted.
　　I myself will give you away.

MOLLY: Oh no you won't, nor the Sergeant, nor Mr New-
　　　some.
　　And that's the reason why we're leaving town.
　　I'll not go empty-handed for I've a promise,
　　Made on a bible, of very substantial money.

INSPECTOR: I've money enough to keep a wife in comfort.

SERGEANT: If we'd known long ago that Molly had money
　　She'd not be single now.

INSPECTOR: You have no soul for love. Your uniform
　　Is a strait-jacket to the heart.

SERGEANT: Well, damn your strait-jacket. I could tell you
　　　things.

MOLLY [*sweetly*]: But you won't, Sergeant. Think of your
　　　stripes.

INSPECTOR: We must be going soon. Justice O'Hanlon,
　　This was the strangest day. I've been bewildered,
　　Frightened, enraged, and finally in love.
　　In spite of all I can truthfully report
　　At least one Court where Law and Justice are
　　Administered by a man in love with both,
　　And one who though he's suffering and tired

And old and wounded can still play his part.
You never told me how you got that dart.

JUSTICE: An honourable scar won in the war for right;
   As I was walking in the snow last night
   A fearful fiend with eyes as red as port
   A tail and cloven hooves, came from the Court
   And tempted me to sin.

INSPECTOR: How monstrous.

JUSTICE: He was a monster of the ancient kind
   Who offered me all gifts that come to mind
   If I would do injustice, fix a case
   That's pending. He even offered me a place
   Among the highest princes of the pit,
   Eternal youth, if I would but acquit
   A damned soul who will appear next week
   Charged with unmentionable crimes I dare not speak.
   Sergeant you know the case?

SERGEANT: The case? Oh . . . Oh . . . Oh course, of course.

JUSTICE: I called on Patrick, scourge of snakes and devils,
   Who purified our isle of all such evils,
   And in an instant there was war between
   The Demon and the Powers of Good, unseen.
   There on the snow they struggled, but a blow
   From that black monster struck and laid me low.

CLERK: You should have seen his wounded head this morning.

INSPECTOR: All this explains the footsteps in the snow.

JUSTICE: Of course, of course, I should have thought of that.
   I knew no more, and when I woke again
   The Saint and Devil had vanished from the plain,
   But from the princely stars there came a strain
   Of perfect music that seemed like heavenly rain.

INSPECTOR: And yet you modestly concealed this story
   Which surely guarantees immortal glory.

JUSTICE: Ten fights like this will not repulse the Devil;
   Our fight is endless against the Powers of Evil.

INSPECTOR: Cloonmore indeed is blessed in such a man
    Ridding it of the imps and spies of Satan.
JUSTICE: Such fights are rare, especially in Cloonmore,
    This little paradise at heaven's door,
    Where all are satisfied, and you take home
    A lovely bride, new-risen from the foam.
    [*He gestures towards the Botticelli picture and then towards*
    MOLLY.]
INSPECTOR: Do you think it quite right, Justice, to have such
    pictures?
    In a government office they'd certainly earn strictures.
JUSTICE: When Molly's left us I'll surely take it down
    And hang instead a sober study in brown.
    Yet you might thank it, for I can say between us,
    Without that rise there'd be no Mount of Venus.
INSPECTOR [*consternated*]: Then you were listening?
JUSTICE: To what? I mean
    That Venus unborn could not be love's sweet queen.
    So Sergeant, take her down.
    [*The* SERGEANT *stands on a chair and takes down the pic-*
    ture. The JUSTICE *hands it to the* INSPECTOR, *who accepts*
    it gingerly.]
JUSTICE: Since you've the daughter, you must have the mother;
    It will be long till we see such another.
    And so all's ended.
INSPECTOR: All except the case.
JUSTICE [*puzzled*]: The case? Oh yes, O'Sullivan and Duffy.
    That's settled, since O'Sullivan marries Duffy.
    We'll strike it from the records and forget
    That such antagonists had ever met.
    Sergeant, collect the Inspector's wig and gown,
    Newsome, you will take the Inspector down
    And see his car has petrol, oil and water;
    Take Venus too, I'll wait here with her daughter.
    [*They all go. At the door the* INSPECTOR *turns.*]

INSPECTOR: Good-bye and thanks.

JUSTICE: Good-bye, Inspector.

INSPECTOR: This is the greatest day of all my life.
  To meet your Honour and to win a wife;
  And what a wife, a true Penelope
  Who waited for me though she never saw me.

JUSTICE: Hurry before the snow comes on again.

INSPECTOR: Good-bye. Good-bye. Parting is such sweet
  pain. [*Exit.*]

JUSTICE [*to* MOLLY]: Get him away before Julia returns.
  And when will you return?

MOLLY: Never.

JUSTICE: Never? You'll surely not stay with a gawk like
  that?

MOLLY: He's my man now.

JUSTICE: But that was all an act
  To save me, and to keep your solemn pact.

MOLLY: You'll do your part now; I've salvaged your career.

JUSTICE: You're far too good for him; you must stay here.

MOLLY: He is too good for me. I'll be his wife
  And I'll be good and faithful all my life.
  But if you say one word I'll have him down
  To take the lid off you and Cloonmore town.
  It's up to you to handle Julia's case,
  Give her ten pounds and try to save your face.
  But one more trick like Teazie's and I'll see
  That there's a new Justice here immediately.

JUSTICE: But all I ever wanted was a kiss.

MOLLY: Kisses can be expensive – so take this.
    [*She kisses him lightly.*]
  Perhaps the last kiss.

JUSTICE: Perhaps the last kiss that I will ever get.
  For aged Romeo no Juliet.
    [*A car horn sounds.*]

MOLLY: Good-bye, good-bye, it's time for me to go.

JUSTICE: Juliet must not detain her Romeo.

[*She kisses him again lightly and runs out. He stands looking out through the window.*]

JUSTICE: Last kisses, last farewells, at what a cost
Is safety bought. What's gained, and what is lost?
To be a swaggering youngster for an hour
I could abandon money, place, and power;
I'd give up all I have without a pain
To tramp it barefoot and be in love again. . . .
But still that louser's gone – I can't complain.

CURTAIN